 here is enormous concern today about the federal budget, and almost all of it begins and ends with the deficit as *the* problem. But eminent economist Herbert Stein argues *Governing the $5 Trillion Economy*, the solutions most often proposed are escapist. Freezes, across-the-board cuts, or constitutional amendments all fail to take into account the real needs of the nation and focus too narrowly on the federal budget as an end in itself.

Stein cuts through the stalemated and aimless discussion of how to divide up the trillion dollars of expenditure in the federal budget and how to pay for it. He focuses attention on the nation's basic objectives—such as economic growth, national security, provision for the very poor, the health and education of the nation and the living standards of the general population—and asks us to consider how the $5 trillion of national output of goods and services should be used, privately and publicly, to achieve those objectives. The decisions about the budget—how much to spend for various programs, what kinds of taxes to impose, and how much deficit to run—are means for reaching the fundamental ends, and decisions about the means should be adapted to the ends. The decision about the deficit, for example, should be adapted to the priority we give to increasing private investment, because the government deficit affects private investment, and through that, economic growth. Stein does not suggest that the government's control over the economy should be expanded. His book is a call for the government to exercise its inevitable influence more rationally, and for private citizens to demand more responsible action from government.

Stein's book is the product of fifty years of observing and participating in the making of economic policy in Washington—mainly as a research economist outside the government but also as member and Chairman of the President's Council of Economic Advisers. His book *The Fiscal Revolution in America* is the classic study of the development of budgeting as it stood twenty years ago, still under the shadow of the depression of the 1930s. His new book points the way that budget policy must go to meet the conditions of the 1990s and beyond.

GOVERNING THE
$5 TRILLION ECONOMY

GOVERNING THE $5 TRILLION ECONOMY

HERBERT STEIN

A TWENTIETH CENTURY FUND ESSAY

New York   Oxford
OXFORD UNIVERSITY PRESS
1989

Oxford University Press

Oxford   New York   Toronto
Delhi   Bombay   Calcutta   Madras   Karachi
Petaling Jaya   Singapore   Hong Kong   Tokyo
Nairobi   Dar es Salaam   Cape Town
Melbourne   Auckland
and associated companies in
Berlin   Ibadan

Published by Oxford University Press, Inc.,
200 Madison Avenue, New York, New York 10016

Oxford is a registered trademark of Oxford University Press

Library of Congress Cataloging-in-Publication Data

Stein, Herbert, 1916–
   Governing the $5 trillion economy.

   "A Twentieth Century Fund Essay."
   Includes index.
   1. Budget—United States. 2. Fiscal policy—United
States. I. Title. II. Title: Governing the five trillion
dollar economy.
HJ2051.S74   1989   339.5'2'0973   88-34531
ISBN 0-19-506038-5

Printing (last digit): 9 8 7 6 5 4 3 2 1

Printed in the United States of America
on acid-free paper

For Mildred

The Twentieth Century Fund is a research foundation undertaking timely analyses of economic, political, and social issues. Not-for-profit and nonpartisan, the Fund was founded in 1919 and endowed by Edward A. Filene.

Foreword

The budget deficit looms large in both the political and public imagination. President-elect Bush is being pressed by editorial-page writers, the Democratic majority in Congress, and such bipartisan bodies as the National Economic Commission to elevate the deficit to the top of his agenda. And there is reason for concern. At $155 billion it absorbs savings that would otherwise be productively invested in the economy, an economy challenged from the East by Japan and from the West by the Europe of 1992.

But as Herbert Stein, senior scholar at the American Enterprise Institute and former chief of the Council of Economic Advisers in the Nixon administration, persuasively argues in the following pages, the deficit is not the problem. The problem is that we do not make good use of the enormous income the American economy generates. We do not do so in large part because we do not think about the problem realistically and pragmatically. Rather than considering the deficit, or for that matter taxes and expenditures in and of themselves, we need to consider them in terms of what they do; specifically, we have to consider them in terms of their effects on the allocation of the national output.

Stein's major recommendation is that the federal budget process should start with decisions about the allocation of this output among its major uses. That is, we should start by budgeting the $5 trillion GNP before we start budgeting the $1 trillion federal expenditures. Such a strategy would force us to become clearer about what is most important to us as a nation. It would also help to bring home the fact that if we want more of something, for example, defense, we will have to take less of something else, for example, health.

Stein is admirably restrained in separating out his preferences for the budget from the budget process he is advocating. At a time when discussions of fiscal policy are all too shrill and partisan, his argument is a model of dispassionate clarity and rigor. The Fund is justifiably proud of having supported it.

Marcia Bystryn, ACTING DIRECTOR
The Twentieth Century Fund
December 1988

Contents

Preface

This book is an elaboration of a few basic facts:

1. The federal government, through its budget and in other ways, is profoundly influencing the uses of the national output—not only the uses contained in the budget but also private uses. It is affecting how much goes for private investment, how much for consumption by the poor, how much for consumption by the nonpoor, and so on.

2. The consequences of public policy for the allocation of the national output among these uses—private and public—are legitimate and actual objects of national concern. We do and should care how much total investment is, and what the condition of the poor is, for example.

3. The government should try to learn more about, and pay more attention to, the consequences of its actions.

To adapt policy to these facts will be difficult, as will be seen from the suggestions in this book. There is no reason to think that it should be easy. We are talking about managing a $1 trillion budget in a nearly $5 trillion economy. That will not be done well with the concepts, procedures, and information that may have been adequate for a much smaller and less pervasive government. Neither will it be done well by following a few simple rules-of-thumb. We find ourselves in the pilot seat of a 747 airliner at thirty-two thousand feet. We had better try to learn to fly.

Readers will not find in this book a prescription for balancing the budget. Balancing the budget is not the name of the game. The name of the game is making good use of the national output, which may or may not involve balancing the budget. By good use of the national output I do not mean my preferred use. I mean a use of the national output in which the government's influence emerges from a better-informed process than the present one.

Some readers of this book may be surprised by it and say, "That's Planning!"—with a capital P. More careful readers, including any who know my previous work, will see that I propose no increase in the powers and responsibilities of government. I would like to see the government do less in many dimensions. But I accept the fact that the federal government is going to be very big, and I would like to see it be better.

Having lived in Washington for fifty years, I believe that I am not naive about the capabilities of government. But it is also naive to think that government, alone of human institutions, is incapable of improvement. I believe that I have seen improvements and that they are still going on, even in the budget process, although not so far and so fast as would be desirable.

In any case, I do not think that "government"—if that means the people inside the Washington Beltway—is the main problem or the main hope. That government operates within the limits of what the public expects or will tolerate. For improvement of public policy, we have to rely on more informed, objective, and honest discussion in the private sector. My hope is that this book will contribute to such discussion.

* * *

I was greatly assisted in the preparation of this book by Glenn Follette. He did much quantitative work, only part of which appears here but all of which influenced me, and he explained to me much recent writing by economists that I would otherwise have found incomprehensible. I have benefited from learned and insightful suggestions by Rudolph Penner and George von

Furstenberg, neither of whom is responsible for anything said here. Gretchen Chellson dealt patiently with several messy drafts.

I am grateful to the American Enterprise Institute for Public Policy Research and its president, Christopher DeMuth, for providing office and library facilities while I worked on this book and for the opportunity to discuss various issues with colleagues there. The Twentieth Century Fund, through its late director, Murray Rossant, provided financial support and encouragement without which this project would not have been undertaken and completed.

Herbert Stein

• 1 •
Understanding the Problem

There is an enormous amount of talk about the federal budget these days. Much of the talk, in and out of government, is defeatist and escapist. It despairs of making rational, informed choices through the political process and seeks, insofar as it seeks any solution, to bypass that process or handcuff it through freezes, across-the-board expenditure cuts, or constitutional amendments. Almost all of this talk begins and much of it ends with the deficit as *the* problem.

I reject the diagnosis, the despair, and the proposed "solutions." My book suggests that we should identify the real problem, and that if we identify it we can make progress toward solving it. The deficit is not the real problem, and as long as we start with doing something about the deficit as the goal we will not make progress, and probably do little about the deficit either.

The problem is this:

The United States is a very rich country. But even a country as rich as the United States cannot do everything its citizens would like it to do, individually or collectively. Decisions must be made about how the overall national income is allocated— how much goes for health, how much for education, how much for investment in plant and equipment, how much for defense, how much for consumption (by whom and for what particular goods and services), and so on. These decisions are vitally important for the national security, for future incomes and living standards, and for the quality of life in America, including the sense of equity and social cohesion.

In the United States, these decisions are mainly made by private individuals who decide how to spend their incomes. They are also partly made by state and local governments. But these decisions are also profoundly influenced by the actions of the federal government. The federal government exercises this influence primarily through the budget. It is not only that the federal government spends about $1 trillion a year, almost one-fourth of the gross national product. It is also, and this is the critical point, that the government's budget greatly affects all kinds of private expenditures. Its deficit affects private investment; its tax treatment of medical expenditures affects private expenditures for health; its loan programs affect private expenditures for education. The list is long.

Moreover, federal influence on private spending is not confined to the budget. Federal regulations influence all kinds of private expenditures—for environmental protection, health and safety, and many other things. Even the president's speeches—his use of the bully pulpit—influence the allocation of the national output.

This influence of the federal government is going to continue. How influential it should be is a matter of controversy. Many people would like to see it reduced, although a significant decrease is extremely unlikely. After all, the Reagan administration was more devoted to reducing the federal influence than any other administration in this century, and its net effect was small if not zero. The federal influence will not be reduced to unimportance.

This pervasive influence is not being exerted well. It is not resulting in an allocation of the nation's output to achieve the main goals of the American people.

Budgeting the Gross National Product

The problem, then, is to improve federal decisionmaking, mainly in the budget but also in other areas of policy, to achieve a better allocation of the national output. It means regarding the federal government as "budgeting the GNP," where budgeting the budget becomes an instrument for doing that. It means deciding—at a certain level of generality of course, and not in detail—how the nearly $5 trillion of the GNP should be allocated and then deciding what budgetary and other policies will help bring about that allocation.

Looking at the budgetary problem as one of budgeting the GNP has three major advantages:

1. The allocations of the GNP come closer to what we are ultimately interested in than the allocations of the budget. If we are interested in the educational attainment of the American people, we have to think about total expenditures for education—private, state, and local as well as federal. We can make sensible decisions about the adequacy of federal expenditures only in the context of total expenditures for our education goals. If we are interested in future economic growth, we have to think about the totality of growth-promoting uses of the national output—which are predominantly private expenditures—and then about the federal policies, including the federal deficit or surplus, that affect that totality. By budgeting the GNP, we can create a bridge between national objectives and budget decisions.

2. Budgeting the GNP helps to bring home the basic fact that if we want more of something we have to take less of something else. If we look only at the claims on the federal budget, it always seems possible to meet more of everyone's claims without sacrificing any, just by increasing the budget. This is not true of the GNP; we cannot simply decide to make the GNP bigger.

3. By looking at the allocation of the GNP, it is also possible to see the nonbudgetary ways in which the federal government influences the allocation of the national output. These nonbudgetary influences are of increasing importance. As the government feels increasingly constrained by the budget situation, there is more and more temptation to achieve the same objectives by nonbudgetary means—thereby concealing the costs that would have been evident if the budget had been used. For example, the idea of achieving national health insurance by mandating the pro-

vision of health care by employers has been under constant consideration. Under the plan, the expenditures would not appear in the budget, and the population would pay through higher prices or lower wages rather than through taxes. Such devices would not, however, take the costs or benefits of the program outside the GNP.

Although the federal budget problem could always be viewed as a problem of allocating the national output among competing uses, that did not become the necessary way to look at it until the 1970s. Before that, the problem could be looked at as having two parts—dividing the national output between federal and other uses and dividing up the federal uses. That was good enough as long as the distinction between federal uses and other uses was clear and as long as the size of the federal sector was small enough that its operation did not greatly affect the allocation of the nonfederal part of the national output.

It is worth recalling that in 1929 federal expenditures were 3 percent of the GNP and that most of that went to defense, veterans' benefits, and interest on debt incurred during World War I. After World War II, in 1948, federal expenditures were 12 percent of the GNP. Expenditures outside the traditional areas (defense, veterans' benefits, interest, international affairs, administration of justice, and general administration) were less than 2 percent of the GNP.

The critical changes came in the 1960s and 1970s. Federal activity spread into a number of fields where its influence had previously been minor—health, education, provision for the poor. By 1978, federal expenditures outside the traditional areas were 13 percent of the GNP, whereas traditional expenditures were only 8 percent. In addition, federal commitments were made to future expenditures in anticipation of further growth of the economy. After 1973, that rate of growth slowed down significantly, well below what had been assumed when many of the commitments had been made. Competition for shares of the federal budget became tighter.

This situation is commonly described as one in which competition for shares of the federal budget became intense, or, even a little more generally, that the budget position became tighter. But the important point is that the competition (i.e., the choices that had to be made) was about uses of the GNP, not about uses of the budget. There was no limit to the size of the budget. There was a limit to the size of the GNP. The key fact was that after 1973 the rate of growth of the GNP could not accommodate the investment needed for previous growth rates to continue as well as for the defense program needed for the national security, the rising provisions for health care embodied in national policy, the educational expenditures consistent with generally held aspirations, and the rise of average consumption levels that recent history had led Americans to expect and that had, to a considerable extent, been underwritten by federal programs, such as Social Security. Some scaling down of these claims was inevitable. Government decisions would greatly affect which of these claims would be met and which would not.

From 1973 to 1980, budget decisions concentrated restraint on defense and private investment. Government defense expenditures as a share of the GNP were reduced. Private investment as a share of GNP was also reduced primarily as a consequence of an increase in the federal budget deficit as a percentage of the GNP, which reduced the supply of savings available to finance private investment. Government decisions helped to promote an increased allocation of the GNP to health care. Also federal policy supported an increase in the share of GNP going to private consumption other than health. It did this by reducing *net* federal taxes relative to the GNP. Although federal taxes increased as a share of the GNP, mainly as an unnoticed consequence of inflation, which pushed taxpayers into higher brackets, federal transfer payments increased even more.

By 1981, this trend in the allocation of the national output no longer seemed sustainable. Defense reductions were causing a dangerous weakening of our military posture, and income earners were opposed to shifting so large a part of their earnings through taxes to recipients of transfer payments, such as Aid to Families with Dependent Children. The national output was reallocated.

A larger share of the GNP went to defense. The share going to private consumption was further increased by reducing net taxes, this time by reducing taxes (relative to the GNP) while holding transfers constant. Federal programs also tended to continue the increase in the share of consumption expenditures going for health. But the increases had to be matched by a reduction somewhere else, and that was in the share going to investment, again by an increase in the deficit (relative to the GNP).

It is a basic premise of this book that current budget processes are not allocating the national output well. By that I do not mean simply that the national output is not being allocated according to my priorities. I will not conceal the fact that the present allocation does not fit my personal preferences. I think we are devoting too little to defense, investment, education, and care for the very poor and too much to health care and the consumption of the nonpoor. But I would not regard my dissatisfaction as evidence that the process is not working. Different people have different priorities, not all of which can be satisfied. A compromise has to be reached, and we have a system for doing that. It is entirely possible that the best compromise is found and yet most or even all people feel dissatisfied.

The reason for believing that we have not achieved the best allocations of the national output, or of the budget, is that the decisions were not based on the best possible information. Even if we accept that everyone in the decisionmaking process is attempting to satisfy his own goals, the outcome will not be the best possible compromise, except by accident, if no one has a correct idea of what his own goals are or how budget decisions affect them. To be more specific, a budget compromise is unlikely to be the correct one if significant actors think that tax increases reduce revenue, that Social Security beneficiaries only receive what they pay for, or that national defense expenditures absorb 40 percent of the GNP. Budget compromise is unlikely to be correct if the decisionmakers have not the slightest idea of the real consequences of budget deficits. The proof that we are not making the right decisions is the abundant evidence that the existing compromises are not reached by a reasoned and informed process.

Information as the Key

If this analysis is correct, it points to the direction in which improvement must be sought. It points to the need for a more reasoned, better-informed process.

The problem of government policy, and of budget policy, is to get good decisions made by officials who are not selected for their decisionmaking ability, whose own interests may not be in making good decisions, and who have inadequate information regarding the probable outcomes of their decisions. "Good decisions" serve the interests of the electorate, who also have inadequate information about the relationship between government policies and their personal interests.

Improving the decisionmaking process requires better people and better information. I shall concentrate on the information aspect; if it is possible to select better officials or to improve the quality of voters, I do not know how to do that, except insofar as improving information may help.

I shall concentrate on two subjects:

1. What decisionmakers, including the electorate, should know

2. How this information can be gotten into the hands and minds of decisionmakers

One must recognize that much of the relevant information will be exceedingly difficult to obtain. Indeed, the most relevant information will be impossible to get. The relevant information is about the relation between policies and outcomes. This information, in principle, exists at different levels. We can ask: (a) What is the relation between a certain government program and national expenditures for health? (b) What is the relation between national expenditures for health and the health of the nation? and (c) What is the relation between the health of the nation and some "ultimate" objective, whether that is visualized as the welfare of the decisionmaker (voter, congressman, or president) or the "national welfare"? This last question cannot be answered: individuals cannot even answer much simpler questions in any objective way, let alone important policy issues. Thus, if A and B disagree about whether it is better to reduce the risk of Soviet domination by x percent or to reduce the proportion of people below the poverty line by y percent, there is no way to resolve that, although discussion may reveal that they do not really disagree.

Nevertheless, some things can be done to improve the quality of information used in the decisionmaking process. The decisions we make imply all kinds of beliefs about relevant relationships. Getting these beliefs out into the open, subject to scrutiny and discussion, will improve results. Decisionmakers, from presidents to voters, should be encouraged to be candid about their ultimate, or almost ultimate, objectives. Presidents should know that their decisions involve sacrificing some things for other things. They should know that their choices are among ends (e.g., private investment or private consumption) and not just among instruments (e.g., taxes or deficits). Other decisionmakers, including citizens, should recognize the priorities that underlie their own policy choices. And all participants in the decisionmaking process should reveal the priorities underlying their policy preferences so that the voting, logrolling, and whatever else goes on will be as informed as possible.

The possibility of learning, that is, of obtaining better information, is greater with respect to the more instrumental questions. What do particular government policies do to the allocation of the national output? How does that allocation affect national health or national security or the condition of the poor? The first step is to acknowledge the importance of such questions. I have no illusions about the possibility of ever answering such questions with complete precision and certainty. That is not required. What is required, and possible if more effort is devoted to it, is improving the quality of the answers. In fact, of course, we are giving answers now, and cannot avoid doing so, but we are not even utilizing the information we already have.

The underlying assumption is that improved information will result in improved outcomes. There are people who would deny this or who would argue that each decisionmaker already has all the information needed to achieve his objectives. To an outside observer, what seems like a lack of information may only reflect a difference of interest. If a congressman voting on an increase in Social Security benefits seems to ignore the consequences of that vote for the year 2037, that may mean that he knows the consequences and doesn't care, or that he doesn't know the consequences because he doesn't care.

The argument that decisionmakers have all the information they need seems inadequate, in government as in the private sector. First, decisionmakers cannot be expected to obtain all the information they need unless they know what information they need. They are not born with that knowledge, nor do they automatically acquire it with their offices. In their effort to obtain new information, they are limited by what they already know. Information injected from the outside may change their idea of what they need to know. No president ever thought he needed to learn anything about the deficit multiplier until Keynes came along.

Second, some information is a public good. Its benefits cannot be confined to those who first acquire it because it is only worth acquiring if it can be made generally available. For example, it is not worthwhile for the congressman from Bedford-Stuyvesant to inform himself, all alone, about the effects of textile import quotas on his constituents. But if the information is provided free, he and others may be influenced. That is one of the reasons for think tanks supported by public-spirited people and receiving tax subsidy.

The budget-reform movement in the United States, now almost eighty years old, has always been primarily about information. Originally, it sought to ensure that when the president and the Congress made decisions about particular items in the budget they had before them information about all the items. Just after World War II, much attention was given to arranging budget information so that it would better reveal the relations among expenditures for particular items and agencies and the common objectives they served. This effort was most developed in the defense program, where there was a need for more information on the expenditures for high-level objectives (strategic deterrence, conventional capability, transportation), which necessitated new consolidation and analysis of the information previously available.

The effort to provide decisionmakers with information relating decisions to objectives—to the outcomes they are interested in—has not kept pace with the great expansion in the past forty years in the size and scope of government and the variety of its instruments. Our present situation is similar in some respects to the situation that existed at the end of World War II, when the Employment Act of 1946 was enacted. The experience of the 1930s had demonstrated that we had a great national problem—unemployment—and that government policy had a great deal to do with its solution. The Employment Act of 1946 declared that it was the policy of the federal government to use its instruments to try to solve the problem, and it created machinery—the Economic Report of the President, the Council of Economic Advisers, and the Congressional Joint Committee on the Economic Report—to focus the attention of policymakers on unemployment. Although at the time some people thought they knew the answer to the problem, the act deliberately did not specify a solution. It only tried to stimulate thinking and research.

Today we have a different serious problem. Although we are a very rich country, we are not allocating our resources well. The government's decisions have a major influence on this allocation, but we are not making these decisions well and are not even recognizing the problem for what it is. The first and most important message of this book is that attention and thought need to be focused on this problem.

Progress does not depend primarily on the goodwill and intelligence of public officials, although one should not despair of that. Private leaders have an important role to play in improving the budget process and may be less inhibited by political considerations than public officials are. In fact, earlier improvements, such as the creation of the executive budget almost seventy years ago, came from private initiatives. Similarly, if today the private sector would talk and think about the budget in an informed and responsible way, public officials would have to follow its lead. What is essential is that a sufficient number of people agree that something needs to be done.

The country is not facing an immediate crisis, unlike the situation that existed at the end of World War II, when fear of a return to depression stimulated new thinking and new institutions for making economic policy, including budget policy. What is involved today is whether the misallocation of our large national output, as a result of mistaken national policy, endangers the national security and the quality of life in America in the future— not next year or the year after but in the next decade or two. If that is not a real possibility, then there is no need for any serious change in budget policy or in the budget process. But if it is a real possibility, as I think it is, and if enough people share that belief (even though their vision of the danger may be different from mine), then the will for substantial improvement may be found.

Improving budget decisions so that they better serve national objectives is the main budget problem today, but not the only one. At least two others may be distinguished:

1. Problems in the allocation of the national output at a lower level of generality, which might be called microallocation problems or "efficiency" problems. There are numerous levels of generality: the allocation of resources between the navy and the air force would be a microdecision in this classification but at a quite high level of generality. The allocation of resources between research on cranberry production and research on raisin production would be a microdecision at a lower level.

There are undoubtedly many inefficiencies in making microallocations, but no enterprise, public or private, ever achieves "ideal" efficiency. What can be done to improve the microdecisions in the budget should be done, but no efforts in that sphere will contribute as much, in my opinion, to solving our national problems as will better decisions about the budget as an allocator of the national output among the "grand" divisions of its uses. In any case, this book will not deal with the microissues.

2. Problems in managing the budget to contribute to the stability of the economy—to maintain employment at a high level and to avoid inflation, or at least to avoid destabilizing effects. Forty years ago, this was the main preoccupation of economists and many others in thinking about the budget. Attention was focused on whether and how and when and by how much to vary expenditures, taxes, deficits, and surpluses to stimulate the economy at some times and to restrain it at others. This problem has not gone away, and I shall discuss it in a later chapter. But it no longer has the centrality it once did. Economic analysis and some experience suggest that short-term variations in the budget position have less effect on the stability of the economy than was once thought. Moreover, prescribing rules that will maximize the contribution of budget policy to economic stability turns out to be very difficult, while the danger of making highly destabilizing errors seems smaller than was once feared.

*   *   *

In what follows, I make a sharp distinction between the problem of using the budget as an allocator of the national output and the problem of adapting the budget to the instability of the economy. Most of the book is devoted to the former problem. Part I reviews the historical background of budget policy from the standpoint of its allocation function, examines some of the key issues, suggests a reform of budget procedures intended to improve the quality of allocational decisions, and applies this suggested approach to the budget decisions facing the country in the 1990s. Part II briefly reviews the development of ideas and practice about the management of the budget from the standpoint of economic stability, considers some of the relevant issues, and suggests a strategy for dealing with them.

Part I
Budgeting the
National Output

• 2 •
Origins of Budget Reform

The history of thinking about budgeting as a process of allocating scarce resources among competing uses seems to begin in 1911. In that year, the Commission on Economy and Efficiency appointed by President Taft (thus known as the Taft commission) issued its report. With it, we enter the modern era of budgeting.

The situation prior to that is something of a mystery. The usual description is that, except in wartime, the federal government did not live with scarcity. The main source of revenue was the import tariff, which was commonly regarded as a benefit to Americans rather than as a burden, and claims on the federal government were limited, so expenditures did not strain the revenue. By 1836, budget surpluses had extinguished the federal debt incurred during the War of 1812, and the government did not know what to do with its money. It solved the problem by returning some to the states. (Apparently, Parkinson's Law, which says that expenditures rise to meet revenues, was not yet operative.) A similar embarrassment occurred in the 1890s. Under the National Banking Act, enacted during the Civil War, National Bank notes were secured by federal debt. But by the end of the century, budget surpluses had so reduced the debt that there was not enough debt to support the currency needed by the growing economy. Despite this apparent budgetary ease, the century was marked by a continuing struggle between the Congress and the executive over control of expenditures, suggesting that there was not enough to satisfy everyone.

The Taft commission was part of the general reform, good-government, movement of the early twentieth century. It probably also reflected a feeling that revenue was becoming scarce, as evidenced by the introduction at this time of the federal income tax (actually reintroduction, since there had been a federal income tax during the Civil War).

Among the recommendations of the Taft commission, three are particularly relevant here:

1. The president should submit a unified, comprehensive budget, covering both revenues and expenditures. Previously, the spending departments had submitted separate appropriation requests, and the Treasury had submitted revenue estimates. The purpose of the unified presidential budget was to bring about a weighing of the expenditures against one another.

2. Expenditures should be classified according to their purposes, not only according to the organization that makes them, in order to help evaluate their contribution to national objectives.

3. Budget decisions should be decentralized, so the president and the Congress would make the largest and most general decisions; lower-level decisions would be made by lower-level officials who would be better informed about matters under their jurisdictions.

Action on the recommendations of the Taft commission was deferred by World War I. When legislation was finally enacted in 1921, it carried out only the first recommendation: the president was required to submit a unified budget, and a Bureau of the Budget was created—in the Treasury at that time—to assist him. The presidents of the 1920s—Warren Harding, Calvin Coolidge, and Herbert Hoover—used this new authority to carry out their primary objectives: to hold down government expenditures and to lay the basis for tax reduction. However, they did not create any process for systematically obtaining the best information to make the best choices among expenditure programs.

In a sentence that sounds eerily familiar today, Arthur Smithies says of that period: "But we can say that the President's decisions were arbitrary, that the Army and Navy felt they were cut to an unwarranted extent, and that hindsight does not prove the Army and the Navy to have been wrong."[1]

Two reform ideas from the 1920s remain of interest today, even if only as a reminder of the cycle in thinking about the budget. One is that the government did not merely accept the idea of balancing the budget as conventional wisdom. It made a deliberate decision to do more than that, and to reduce the debt from World War I. A fund was established for retiring the debt, and payments into it were part of the expenditure side of the budget. "Balancing the budget" meant what we would today call running a surplus. This posture was facilitated by the expectation of repayment of loans from our European allies, which the United States could then use to repay its debt. The point is that an answer was given to the question of the proper relation between revenues and expenditures; the answer was that revenues should exceed expenditures.

The second idea worth recalling is that tax reduction was not only a way of giving money back to taxpayers; it was also believed to raise the national income, with the result that the loss of revenue would be less than if the national income had been held constant. This idea is mainly associated with Andrew W. Mellon, who was secretary of the treasury during the 1920s. This idea remained part of Republican economic thinking but did not exert much influence on policy again until 1981.

The orderly ways of controlling the budget during the 1920s were drastically altered by the depression and the war. The idea that the budget should be balanced, with regular provision for debt reduction, was one of the first things to go. Ironically, President Hoover, who understood that balancing the budget during a depression was unnecessary and probably counterproductive, nonetheless made a vain effort to do so in 1932, with the hope of restoring the confidence of investors at home and abroad.

In that same year, Franklin D. Roosevelt ran on a platform that criticized Hoover's deficits and promised a balanced budget. As president, he quickly found that he could not do it. He did, however, try to preserve the idea of a balanced budget as a policy objective, probably because he thought his constituents wanted it and possibly because he wanted it as well. The result was that Roosevelt and his team considered a number of ideas for balancing "something"—either balancing the budget over the business cycle, balancing current expenditures while borrowing to finance capital expenditures, or balancing "ordinary" expenditures while borrowing to finance "emergency" expenditures. None of this left any mark except to suggest the slipperiness of the concept of "balancing the budget."

The balanced budget was not the only victim of the depression. Under the pressure of the emergency, Congress gave up a great deal of its control over the direction of expenditures, appropriating large lump sums to the president to spend at his discretion. The first large "trust fund" was established (for Social Security), and it was placed outside the budget. A number of public corporations were started and also placed outside the budget. The comprehensiveness of the budget was substantially compromised.

Two lessons relevant today might have been learned during the depression but were not. One was the difference between the nominal object of an expenditure and its real effect, even its real desired effect. We were spending a lot of money for bridges, dams, and roads, partly because we wanted bridges, dams, and roads but mainly because we wanted people to work. The other lesson was that the real cost of a federal expenditure was not accurately represented by the number of dollars that went into it. In the depression situation, the expenditures were costless. They did not draw resources or output away from other uses. Most likely, they increased the use of other resources and output by increasing total employment and productivity more than the amount absorbed in the direct federal expenditure. These illustrations are drawn from depression conditions, but the basic fact—that the consequences and the costs of government expenditures are seen not in the budget but in the economy—applies in other situations as well, even today.

A similar, generally valid lesson was learned during the war—specifically, some "private" uses of the national output are proper objects of national policy and are affected by the budget or other instruments. The cost of the war was not the dollars raised in taxes or by borrowing but was the output that was diverted from other, nonwar uses. Taxes and borrowing were only part of the means by which this diversion was effected. We were dealing with the entire economy, not only with the budget. There were various kinds of rationing at different levels; there was a strong effort to increase private savings. Moreover, as the rationing reveals, economic policy was concerned not only with the diversion from nonwar uses but also with the composition of the diversion. Some "private" uses—that is, uses of output not paid for in the budget—were of great priority for the war effort and therefore were preferred by the rationing system. The war, like the depression, was an extreme situation, but some of the lessons still hold. For example, the cost of resource uses that are promoted by the government is not the money the government spends but the resource uses that are sacrificed as a consequence of the government's action.

After the war, most of the thinking about the budget focused on the stabilization question, which will be discussed in Part II. But two ideas about the allocation problem, which had been considered in the report of the Taft commission, were revived. The first was the requirement that expenditures and revenues be balanced in order to serve as a discipline on expenditure decisions, thus resisting the tendency of governments to make expenditures whose benefits did not equal their costs. The second was that information about past and proposed expenditures be arranged and presented by programs and functions, rather than through (or in addition to) classification by departments and agencies. The objective was to clarify the relation between expenditures and the national objectives they were supposed to serve. The common illustration was the presentation of the budget for the Department of Defense. The distribution of expenditures among the army, navy, and air force was considered to be much less informative than a distribution among strategic forces, conventional forces, transportation, research, and so on.

It should be noted that the emphasis on balancing the budget did not imply that taxes were really the cost of government expenditures. Neither did it imply anything about the need for balancing the budget or the desirability of doing so, for its own sake. The requirement that expenditures be balanced by taxes was to solve a political problem, not an economic one. The need to raise taxes to pay for expenditures was supposed to bring the costs home to the politicians who were making the expenditure decisions. The underlying idea was that, although the expenditures would have their own costs whether or not paid for in taxes, the politicians would not recognize the costs unless they had to go through the unpleasantness of raising taxes. As far as that logic went, some other requirement could have served the purpose: every congressman could have been required to do ten push-ups for every billion dollars of federal expenditures. The advantage of the balanced-budget requirement over other conceivable disciplines on spending was that the country believed in that requirement—even if economists did not—and politicians would therefore feel obliged to honor it.

The disciplinary value of the balanced-budget requirement was emphasized in the influential 1947 statement "Taxes and the Budget: A Program for Prosperity in a Free Economy" published by the Research and Policy Committee of the Committee for Economic Development. The statement listed four main considerations for the choice of a budgetary policy. The first was that the budget should contribute to economic stability. The second was that:

> Budgetary policy should serve to restrain unnecessary government expenditure and to stimulate efficiency in government. Everyone agrees that economy in government is important. But the achievement of economy requires that our belief in economy be effectively directed against the particular pressures that always will be found in support of particular expenditures. Budgetary policy can be an effective force for economy if we harness the legitimate and specific interest in lower taxes to the general interest in economy. Every pro-

posal that would expand government functions should pass the test of society's willingness to pay for it in taxes.[2]

The committee's interest in the balanced-budget rule for reasons other than maintaining discipline over expenditures was not strong. The statement cited did recommend a moderate budget surplus under conditions of "reasonably high employment and production" in order to reduce the tax burden resulting from interest on the federal debt. However, discussion at the time revealed that the committee was as much motivated by the desire not to shock the conventional wisdom about balancing the budget as by any concerns of its own. A little later, when the committee wrote a statement about managing the federal debt, it started by disclaiming any hope or ambition for a significant reduction in the size of the debt and concentrated instead on questions of its composition and monetization. Later still, when the desire for tax reduction conflicted with the desire for a budget surplus at high employment, it was the surplus that was sacrificed.

A similar emphasis on the balanced-budget rule as discipline is found in a statement of a representative group of economists to the Congressional Joint Committee on the Economic Report in 1949:

> Annual budget-balancing is, thus, both difficult in practice and unsound in principle. But one great merit it does have: it provides a yardstick by which legislators and the people can scrutinize each activity of government, testing it both for efficiency of operation and for its worthwhileness in terms of cost. Every government program undertaken has to be paid for in a clear and unequivocal sense.

Thus, one of the main elements in postwar thinking about the budget as an allocation process was that consideration of the relation between costs and benefits of federal expenditures could be enforced by requiring politicians who raise expenditures to pay a cost. The political onus of raising taxes was to be a surrogate for the real cost of the expenditure decision. The requirement to face the cost would be enforced by the public's devotion to the idea of a balanced budget.

Both the Committee for Economic Development and economists of the time recognized the problem of reconciling this disciplinary link between expenditures and revenues with a stabilizing fiscal policy that rejected the idea that the budget should be balanced every year (or in any particular year or series of years). The CED solution was the "stabilizing budget policy" of setting tax rates so that the budget would be balanced under standard economic conditions but not necessarily under actual economic conditions. This will be discussed in Part II.

Another important postwar idea about managing the budget as an allocating instrument was that information on expenditures should be arranged in such a way as to permit better perception of the relation between the expenditures and the objectives of national policy. This was one of the highlights of the report of the Hoover commission in 1949. As the commission said, "The whole budgetary concept of the Federal government should be refashioned by the adoption of a budget based upon functions, activities and projects: this we designate a 'performance budget.'" Smithies summarized this aspect of the commission's report: "The main interest of performance budgeting is to improve public comprehension of the budget in terms of the policy objectives it is designed to further."[3]

This call for relating expenditures to policy objectives repeated recommendations of the Taft commission, forty years earlier, and was repeated many more times in subsequent years. In fact, in 1949, Congress enacted legislation requiring the president to submit a budget in which expenditures were classified by function, as well as by organization units, beginning with budgets for fiscal 1950. It was a long time, however, probably around 1975, until the functional classification of expenditures became the main way in which Congress looked at and made decisions about the budget. Prior to that, the congressional process focused mainly on the amounts provided for the various departments, bureaus, divisions, and so on.

At the time of the Hoover commission report, the traditional functions of government accounted for about 80 percent of federal expenditures (Figure 2.1 and Figure 2.2). These federal expenditures were almost identical to total national expenditures for

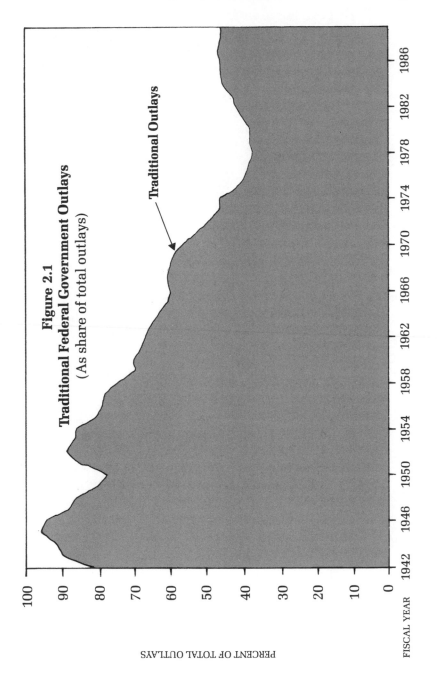

Figure 2.1
Traditional Federal Government Outlays
(As share of total outlays)

Traditional Outlays

PERCENT OF TOTAL OUTLAYS

FISCAL YEAR

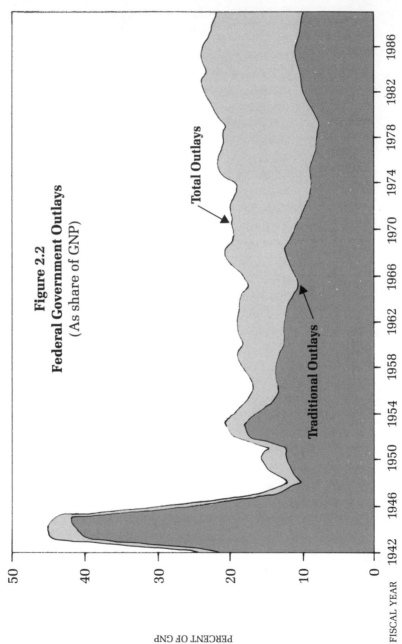

Figure 2.2
Federal Government Outlays
(As share of GNP)

Data for Figures 2.1 and 2.2
Federal Government Outlays

Fiscal Year	Traditional[a] as a Percent of Outlays	Traditional as a Percent of GNP	"NEW"[b] as a Percent of GNP	Total as a Percent of GNP
1942	81.6%	20.17%	4.54%	24.71%
1943	89.9	40.16	4.52	44.68
1944	91.7	41.47	3.73	45.20
1945	95.8	41.83	1.82	43.65
1946	94.5	24.51	1.44	25.94
1947	88.2	13.60	1.82	15.43
1948	86.2	10.35	1.66	12.01
1949	80.6	11.86	2.85	14.72
1950	78.0	12.44	3.51	15.95
1951	85.0	12.28	2.17	14.45
1952	88.9	17.58	2.19	19.77
1953	86.7	18.05	2.77	20.82
1954	86.5	16.58	2.60	19.18
1955	80.8	14.31	3.41	17.71
1956	79.7	13.47	3.43	16.90
1957	79.0	13.73	3.66	17.38
1958	75.2	13.77	4.54	18.30
1959	70.0	13.40	5.73	19.13
1960	70.4	12.81	5.39	18.19
1961	68.3	12.89	5.97	18.86
1962	67.2	12.87	6.29	19.15
1963	66.0	12.49	6.45	18.94
1964	63.6	11.98	6.86	18.84
1965	60.9	10.71	6.87	17.58
1966	60.1	10.95	7.26	18.20
1967	61.0	12.08	7.73	19.82
1968	60.3	12.65	8.32	20.97
1969	59.7	11.80	7.95	19.76
1970	57.2	11.29	8.47	19.76
1971	52.7	10.50	9.40	19.90
1972	49.5	9.90	10.11	20.01
1973	46.7	8.96	10.22	19.17
1974	46.6	8.86	10.16	19.02
1975	42.0	9.17	12.66	21.83
1976	39.6	8.66	13.23	21.89
1977	38.7	8.19	12.98	21.17
1978	37.9	8.00	13.12	21.12
1979	38.6	7.94	12.62	20.57
1980	38.8	8.59	13.54	22.13
1981	40.1	9.10	13.61	22.71
1982	42.3	10.06	13.70	23.76
1983	42.8	10.42	13.91	24.33
1984	45.9	10.60	12.51	23.10
1985	46.1	11.08	12.96	24.04
1986	46.7	11.11	12.68	23.79
1987	47.0	10.69	12.04	22.73
1988 (est.)	46.1	10.35	12.09	22.44
1989 (est.)	46.3	10.08	11.83	21.78

Source: "Historical Tables, Budget of the United States Government: Fiscal Year 1989" (U.S. Government Printing Office, Washington, D.C., 1988).

a. Traditional spending includes outlays for the following functions: defense, veterans' benefits, international affairs, administration of justice, general government, and net interest payments.

b. "New" spending is composed of all other outlays, including: health, education, social security, medicare, income security, energy, natural resources, commerce and housing, community development, agriculture, science, general fiscal assistance, and offsetting receipts.

those functions. Government defense expenditures, for example, which absorbed about 35 percent of the budget (in 1950), essentially were the amount the country spent for defense. In determining how much the federal government should spend for defense, therefore, we were also determining how much of the national output should go for defense.

The same calculation could not be made in all areas. Federal expenditures for health were not equal to total expenditures for health. Whether the federal expenditures were wise or effective could only be judged in the context of how much the nation was spending for health and how that was influenced by what the federal government was doing. Merely to classify an amount of federal expenditure for "health" did not give useful information about what was happening to the national objective "health." In 1950, that was not very important, or at least it did not seem so. Federal health expenditures amounted to only six-tenths of 1 percent of the federal budget and one-tenth of 1 percent of the GNP. But by 1988, federal health expenditures were almost 12 percent of the federal budget and 2.5 percent of the GNP. These expenditures may (as intended) have been having a major effect on the share of the national output devoted to health, but this effect was not visible from the expenditure totals in the budget. Similar statements can be made about federal expenditures for education, transfer payments to the old and the poor, aid to agriculture, research, and so on. Federal expenditures in these nontraditional areas—which amounted to about 3 percent of the GNP in 1950 and have since risen to about 12 percent—cannot be understood except in relation to the national expenditures for those purposes. Thus, the inadequacy of the functional classification of expenditures in the budget was much less important thirty years ago than it is today.

The 1950s concept of "performance budgeting," to use the term of the Hoover commission, was inadequate in other respects as well. Not only expenditures had "functions"; taxes had functions as well, as we discovered later with the introduction of the concept of "tax expenditures." Taxes had an effect on the use of the national output. Some tax provisions very intentionally did quite specific things. For example, the federal income tax exemption of health insurance provided by employers increased the share of the national output devoted to health expenditures as much as direct federal expenditures did. Even where such specific consequences were not directly visible, taxation had a general effect on private consumption. Budget surpluses or deficits also had their functions—commonly described as increasing or decreasing national savings and investment. Government loan and loan guarantee programs had functions that were not well described by the amounts included in the budget, if they were included at all. Similarly, government regulations had functions that were not visible in the budget but that were often substitutes for functions in the budget. Thus, regulations requiring businesses to undertake certain expenditures to clean up the environment could be a substitute for federal expenditures with the same purpose.

The logic of the recommendation that federal expenditures be described in functional terms to clarify their relation with national objectives was not carried to its conclusion. If it were, taxes and borrowing and lending and loan guarantees and regulations would also have been evaluated in terms of their effects on the uses of the national output and, through that, on the achievement of national objectives.

Thus, we were operating in the 1950s and 1960s with two major themes of budget reform. One was that the benefits of spending should be balanced against their costs, which would be represented by the taxes required to balance the budget. The second was that expenditures should be classified by functions or programs so that their relation to policy objectives could be seen. These were both imperfect ideas. The notion that the budget should be balanced and that the requirement to balance it would lead to a reasonable equilibrium between costs and benefits of expenditures rested on no logical foundation. Neither did the idea that the classification of expenditures by "function" would give an adequate picture of the relation between government actions and government policy objectives.

Nevertheless, the operation of the government and the budget during those two decades raised no great problems, or did not seem to do so. Growth of the economy at a faster rate than had been anticipated, plus a little inflation, regularly generated enough additional revenue to permit some amounts of money to be distributed among tax reduction and various claimants on the spending side of the budget, without putting great strain on the principle that the budget should be balanced in times of prosperity. The claims for expenditure were held down by common notions of the proper role of government, aside from the question of the availability of resources. Thus, when President Kennedy wanted to increase federal aid to education, Congress resisted, not on grounds that the government could not afford it but on grounds that the federal government should not be in that business at all.

Perhaps serious mistakes were made in the allocation of the national output during that period. Possibly with more foresight, we would have taken steps to improve education in America before we were shocked by the Soviet *Sputnik*, and perhaps earlier steps to deal with poverty might have forestalled later problems. Such speculation notwithstanding, the budget processes of the 1950s and 1960s were essentially adequate to the needs of the time.

And yet there were signs even then that more realistic, result-oriented thinking about the major budget decisions was needed.

1. In his January 1960 budget message, President Eisenhower said: "In times of prosperity . . . sound fiscal and economic policy requires a budget surplus to help counteract inflationary pressures, to ease conditions in capital and credit markets, and to increase the supply of savings available for productive investment so essential to continued economic growth."

The clause about savings, investment, and economic growth is the classic nineteenth-century economists' argument for a balanced budget or budget surplus. It had not been heard much in the United States. Eisenhower's revival of it was partly a reflection of concern about economic growth in America as Soviet economic growth began to appear more frightening. It may also have resulted from a need to resist demands, mainly from Republicans, for tax reduction. Of course, if the notion that a surplus is desirable in order to add to savings had been pursued, the next question would have been how big the surplus should be, and that would have led to serious rethinking about the budget. But the idea was not pursued.

2. In 1959, President Eisenhower established a Commission on National Goals, with the objective of stimulating and informing national discussion of that subject. Edward Denison and I prepared a paper for the Commission on High Employment and Growth in the American Economy. The paper explained that increasing revenues relative to federal expenditures (excluding capital expenditures) was the most feasible way to increase total national savings and total national investment and provided some estimates of the size of the resulting effect on economic growth. The Denison-Stein paper made no recommendations, however, since its mandate was only to present options. The commission did not recommend generating a budget surplus, however, although it did suggest some other steps to accelerate growth.[4]

3. Professor James Tobin of Yale University wrote a much-discussed article in the *New Republic* in 1960 recommending that the federal government run a budget surplus in order to increase savings, investment, and economic growth. This idea was soon swamped by the drive for tax reduction (as the means to growth and other desired objectives), which reached its peak in President Kennedy's 1962 proposal for tax reduction, while Professor Tobin was a member of the President's Council of Economic Advisers.[5]

4. At the beginning of 1969, the new Nixon administration undertook a fundamental review of the defense program. As part of that review, the Council of Economic Advisers was asked to evaluate the economic consequences of defense programs of substantially different sizes. Instead of concentrating on the conventional questions about the effects of greater or lesser defense

spending on inflation and unemployment, the council tried to estimate the effects on the allocation of the national output. It asked what the effects would be on consumption, housing, other private investment, other federal services, and state-local services. Several options were prepared, on different assumptions about the complementary policies adopted. A similar exercise was attempted in 1970, but by then the differences in the size of the defense programs being contemplated were so small that the crude econometrics available could not distinguish among them.

5. The February 1970 Annual Report of the Council of Economic Advisers devoted a chapter ("Uses of the National Output") to an argument much like the one presented here. It noted that the federal government was involved in influencing the allocation of the national output, not just through its own budget, and should therefore consider explicitly and deliberately what that influence should be. The report said:

> The attention given here to the Federal Government's role in allocating the national output may seem excessive for a nation committed to a free-market, decentralized economic system. The idea that the Federal Government must make hard decisions to allocate the limited resources within its own budget is commonplace. The idea that it does or should influence the allocation of the output of the entire economy is not. However, the Federal Government does have an important influence on decisions about the use of resources in the private, as well as the Government sector. Perhaps that influence should not be as big or as detailed as it is. Nevertheless a large influence exists, and much of it is inevitable or desirable or both. This influence should be recognized, its effects appraised, and decisions consciously made to achieve the effects that are preferred.

The report described these influences on private resource use through taxes, borrowing, lending, and the complementary or substituting relations with federal expenditures. It stated:

> The substance of the priorities problem is to allocate the future national output among alternative uses in a rational way that reflects decisions about national priorities. This tailoring of Federal decisions concerning allocation to a view of national priorities requires—

1. An estimate of what the future national output can be.

2. A view of the claims upon the national output—the things we would like to do with it—that are eligible for serious consideration.

3. A view of the policy measures that would be necessary to bring about satisfaction of some claims rather than others.

4. A decision about the claims that are to be satisfied and the policies to carry out the decision.

Recognizing that "Step 4 in this process must, of course, ultimately reflect government decisionmaking at the highest level," the report proceeded with a tentative approach to the first three steps. It estimated the potential growth of the national output, then calculated the claims that it thought implicit in existing tax and expenditure policies (goals for housing incorporated in existing legislation, trends in the capital/output ratio, past experience with the propensity to consume, and other variables). It then discussed the policies, mainly taxing and spending, that might implement one or another decision about priorities among these claims.

The president's own Economic Report in 1970 called special attention to the problem of allocating the national output and to the council's analysis of that problem in its report. The president said: "I hope it will be studied carefully and its precedent carried forward in future years. That analysis is neutral about which options and claims should be chosen. The purpose of the analysis is to help everyone observe the discipline of keeping claims and plans within the limits of our capacity, and to make sure that excessive claims do not prevent us from achieving our most important goals."

The precedent was not, however, carried forward in future years. The president and the Council of Economic Advisers were soon absorbed in matters more immediate than rethinking the allocation of the national output. But the urgency of the allocation problem was beginning to increase; the council's 1970 report was a reflection of that.

During the 1960s, the country had been living with the idea of a "fiscal dividend"—the increase in revenue (beyond the built-in growth of expenditures) that resulted from the growth of the economy. That dividend was available to pay for new federal programs. By 1969, we were looking forward to the revenue continuously generated by growth as well as to both the fiscal dividend and the Vietnam dividend (i.e., the savings resulting from an after-the-war decline in defense spending). When the Nixon administration came into office, it created a task force (the Interagency Study Group on Post-Vietnam Planning), of which I was chairman, to study the economic problems that would arise with the end of the war, including what to do with the dividend. The task force discovered that there would be no fiscal dividend. The ending of the temporary tax surcharge, plus the expenditure increases built into existing programs (many of which were enacted during the Johnson administration), would exhaust the foreseeable revenue for several years. A report of this finding to the president and the Domestic Council at a meeting in the president's California office later in 1969 led Daniel Patrick Moynihan, director of the Domestic Council, to a remark much-quoted at the time: "The Vietnam dividend is as evanescent as the clouds over San Clemente." The projections contained in the 1970 Council of Economic Advisers' report led to the same conclusion.

The increasingly visible tightness in the budget was one of the reasons for the struggle between President Nixon and the Democratic Congress. The president wanted more defense expenditure than the Congress did; Congress wanted more tax reduction and nondefense expenditure increases than the president did. At one point, the president used what he considered his constitutional authority to impound appropriations made by Congress—that is, not to spend the money. Congressional resentment at this infringement of what it considered its authority and a Supreme Court decision that supported Congress were major factors leading to the Congressional Budget and Impoundment Control Act of 1974, hereafter called the Budget Reform Act.

The 1974 act required the president to spend congressionally appropriated funds unless he followed a specified procedure for congressional approval not to spend them. Further, a congressional mechanism was created to prevent the president from using a residual power to keep the budget under control. And if the president could not exercise a final restraint upon the outcome of the separate decisions of numerous congressional committees approved by Congress without relation to each other, Congress would have to establish some central control itself.

The Budget Reform Act of 1974 made the most comprehensive change in congressional budget procedure in American history. Aside from details, some of which have since been changed, the provisions were:

1. A Budget Committee would be established in each House of Congress.

2. The Budget Committee in each House would recommend a Budget Resolution specifying the amount permitted to be spent in the next fiscal year for each of the main expenditure functions and the amount of revenue to be raised. After consideration of these recommendations, each House would adopt a Budget Resolution. The resolutions of the two Houses would be reconciled and incorporated in a Joint Budget Resolution.

3. The Joint Resolution would serve as binding instructions to the appropriating and revenue-raising committees of the two Houses. Legislative proposals that violated the Joint Resolution could be objected to on a point of order before adoption.

4. A Congressional Budget Office would be established to serve as a staff for the two Budget committees.

A common reaction to the congressional budget process established by the 1974 act has been disappointment. Some of this has been due to procedural failures—deadlines have not been met and there has been frequent use of continuing resolutions lumping all appropriations together, bypassing deliberative processes in Congress and in the White House. But most of the disappointment has been over outcomes. Some of the authors of the legislation thought that the main reason for it was to avoid deficits and, even more important, to limit the growth of expenditures.

Neither of these results was realized. By 1984, deficits had risen to over 4 percent of the GNP, unprecedented in the United States except in times of war. In the early 1980s, outlays were higher relative to the GNP than they had been at any time since World War II. This led some to claim that the act was a failure.[6]

Defenders of the act have attributed these deficiencies to the extraordinarily difficult economic and political conditions with which the new process had to contend. They refer to the slowdown in economic growth, the rise of expenditures required by earlier commitments, and the major difference in priorities between President Reagan and the Congress.[7]

But neither the attacks on nor the defense of the 1974 Budget Reform Act tells the entire story. The detractors assume that there was a congressional policy to hold down deficits and expenditures, which the process (mandated by the act) should have implemented but did not. In fact, no such policy existed, except rhetorically. The process carried out the wishes of Congress. On the other hand, it is also true, as defenders of the process claimed, that political and economic conditions were difficult. Whether or not the process helped Congress make the best adaptation it could to those conditions is debatable; the probable answer is that it did not and that it was insufficient for the problem.

The new process was a logical method for budgetmaking on certain assumptions. The assumptions were that the costs and benefits of government programs could be deduced or appraised from the revenue and expenditure figures. In that case, centralized consideration of revenues and expenditures relative to each other would permit a balancing of overall costs with overall benefits, and consideration of the expenditures for each budget function relative to the expenditures for all other budget functions would permit an informed choice, equating the benefits from the marginal expenditure on each.

The difficulty, as noted several times in this book, was that the information the Congress was debating about did not represent the real choices. The deficit is the clearest example. Hardly anyone in the decisionmaking process had a clear picture of the real consequences of running a deficit. But if there was a choice to make between spending for, say, Medicare, which many desired strongly, and observing an old-fashioned ritual like balancing the budget, the spending would probably win. No budget process would prevent the government from running deficits if no one in the government thought that there were adverse consequences from deficits.

Much the same could be said about taxes. Of course, contrary to a recent perception, no one ever likes to raise taxes, and there are good reasons against raising taxes. But the idea of "no tax increase" became a shibboleth, invested with a symbolic and political significance that prevented a balancing of the costs of higher taxes against the benefits of higher expenditures or lower deficits.

In general, the 1974 act provided a process for balancing expenditures against each other and against revenues, but the balancing turned out to be in large part among symbols rather than among real competing uses of resources.

Of course, after the act as before it, the government's decisions did affect the allocation of the national output and so reflected a view of the nation's priorities. Before 1981, the priorities turned out to be increasing national health expenditures and increasing the consumption of nonpoor recipients of government transfers, especially the aged, at the expense of defense and private investment. After 1981, the priorities changed, to favor defense and increasing the consumption of the nonpoor income earners, at the expense mainly of private investment and, to some extent, low-income transfer recipients.

The low priority given to private investment, before and after 1981, was effected by larger and larger federal deficits as a share of the GNP. By 1985, these deficits were so far out of line with prevailing assumptions and views of propriety that drastic action seemed justified. Thus, new rules and procedures, the Gramm-Rudman-Hollings Act, were imposed on top of the 1974 Budget Reform Act. The 1974 Budget Committee process would no longer annually determine the proper relation between revenues and expenditures in the light of all competing claims. Instead, the size of the deficit would be limited to a five-year path specified in G-R-H, designed to reach a zero deficit. The Budget Committee process would still determine the allocation of expenditures among the major functions, but it would do so under the threat of a distribution of budget cuts specified in G-R-H. The threat was that if the regular process did not bring the deficit to the G-R-H path, expenditure cuts would be automatically divided in equal percentages between defense and a limited category of nondefense expenditures, and equally divided among several thousand programs, projects, and activities within these areas.

The threat was not intended to be exercised. It was intended to force decisions. But the nature of the threat influenced the nature of the decisions. In particular, it assured that defense would bear a large share of the cuts, which turned out to be the case.

Gramm-Rudman-Hollings did not reflect any evaluation of the consequences of running a deficit or of the costs and benefits of reducing the deficit. The five-year path to a balanced budget was entirely arbitrary, and the knowledge of this probably contributed to the subsequent deviations from the path. The provision for automatic cuts, which influenced the cuts actually made, was also arbitrary. It rested on the belief that equal cuts were in some sense equitable and that the pain would be lessened if spread evenly and presumably lightly. But this principle was reflected in G-R-H only in the most superficial way.

If the object of the exercise was to spread evenly the sacrifice of reducing the deficit, then all resource uses other than those to be promoted by the reduction of the deficit should have been cut equally. On the reasonable assumption that the resource use to be promoted by deficit reduction is private investment, that would have called for equal reduction of all other resource uses, the largest of which by far is private consumption. But G-R-H effectively removed private consumption from consideration as a participant in the proposed cuts by excluding from cuts the largest federal transfer programs—mainly Social Security—and making no provision for tax increases.

Despite these inadequacies, G-R-H was a recognition of certain real problems and an attempt to deal with them. Basically, it recognized the need for a decision about deficits that was more farsighted and durable than the ordinary annual process yielded. It also recognized the need to make spending decisions at a higher level of generality than had been the practice. It dealt primarily with categories like defense, entitlements, nondefense discretionary outlays, interest, and a few special cases. A further step toward making decisions at a high level of generality came after the stock market crash of October 19, 1987. This was commonly, although perhaps not correctly, regarded as a sign that more decisive action was needed to reduce the budget deficit. The result was a "summit" agreement on the budget reached between the president and the congressional leadership, setting targets for the fiscal 1988 and fiscal 1989 budgets in terms of revenues and a few categories of expenditures. The novel features of this agreement were the joint high-level White House-congressional negotiations in advance of the president's submission of a budget for fiscal 1989, the inclusion of revenues in the agreement, and the specification of ceilings for expenditures divided into a very few categories.

We have, then, arrived at a process that has a number of desirable features—a multiyear outlook, a focus on macrodecisions, and high-level involvement at the executive and congressional levels. There are, however, two main problems. One is that the process is the outgrowth of a perceived emergency and may not last. The other, and more important problem, is that the process does not require asking or answering the right questions. The process may be capable of yielding good policy, but it is unlikely to do so unless it is specifically tied to what the government is doing—which is allocating the national output—and is supplied with the relevant information for thinking about that.

• 3 •
Key Issues in
Allocation Policy

The suggestion that we try to achieve a more functional, result-oriented, informed budget policy raises a number of fundamental questions. These are questions for which there may be no hard "scientific" answers, but for which some answers must be found and are in fact found, implicitly or explicitly. In this section I indicate the questions, and my thinking on them.

Are the "Rational" Answers Worth Seeking?

This question might seem to belong at the end of the list, but I put it first because many people argue that the search for rational, objective answers to budgetary questions is vain, and that even if they could be found, the ordinary political process would never put them into effect. These people believe that the best that can be done is to shortcut or constrain the political process to avoid its otherwise inevitable excesses, even if it means forgoing theoretically better solutions.

The primary manifestation of this point of view, of course, is the proposal for a constitutional amendment requiring a balanced budget and, in some versions, limiting government expenditures and revenues. Supporters do not maintain that a balanced budget, or total expenditures and receipts confined to a constant percentage of GNP, is the best outcome. Rather, they believe that the possibility of getting better than the mandated outcomes is slight, whatever arguments economists might make or whatever procedural reforms might be adopted. And they believe that the most probable outcome is much worse than the one the constitutional amendment would mandate.

Advocates of a balanced budget cite evidence for their arguments in two parts—a theory of the political process and an interpretation of the experience of the United States. The political theory also has two parts. The first holds that the decision to run a deficit (if it is a decision to impose a burden on anyone, a matter of dispute to which I shall return) is a decision to impose burdens on future generations, and since future generations do not vote, their interests are underrepresented in political decisions. The second is that the beneficiaries of government spending tend to be aware of their benefits and are thus well organized, whereas those who will pay the costs, whether present or future taxpayers or others, are less aware and less organized. The rise of deficits, taxes, and government spending in the United States and elsewhere is taken as proof that these theories are realistic.

I do not find either the theory or the evidence convincing. It is almost certainly true that politicians do not make rational, objective calculations of the optimum size of the budget deficit—if there is such a thing. But their biases are in both directions. They may undervalue future costs, but they are also inhibited by Micawber-like feelings about deficits, and one cannot tell *a priori* which bias is more powerful. Even supporters of a balanced-budget amendment, such as James Buchanan, agree that there was a "fiscal religion" before Keynes. That admission has a number of implications: one is that, even in a democracy, self-interest is not always controlling. It also suggests the possibility that some of the fiscal religion remains, and may still be of sufficient force to prevent political excesses. Finally, it implies that the political outcomes were significantly influenced by an economist—in this case, Keynes—so that they might again be influenced by argument, suggesting the desirability of further discussion on what would constitute a preferable policy. A constitutional amendment would terminate such discussion.

Moreover, American experience does not point to the inevitability of an explosion of the deficit under present decision-making processes. Deficits have been rising relative to GNP for some time, but they only reached extraordinary proportions in the early 1980s, and have since receded. The ratio of debt to GNP, which had been about 100 percent at the end of World War II, declined until it settled down in the high 20 percent range in the 1970s. The Reagan fiscal policy shocked the figure up to about 40 percent, and current estimates, both by the Office of Management and Budget and by the Congressional Budget Office, have the ratio remaining in the low 40s for the next five years or so. Of course, no one can be sure that the ratio will remain at that level, and that may not be the best level in any case, but the evidence does not indicate that ordinary political processes lead to an unending increase in deficits or debts. Ironically, the most pessimistic evidence about the ability to manage the deficit and the debt came in the period of maximum devotion in the White House to the idea of mandating a balanced budget.

The argument that politics makes some expenditures larger than they would be under generally accepted notions of the general welfare is probably valid. But it seems also to be true that political biases make some expenditures too small. Voters do not strongly support expenditures that result in only small benefits to each of many people, even when those benefits are highly beneficial in the aggregate. Politicians also undervalue expenditures whose benefits may be distant in time or place, like defense expenditures and foreign aid. Once this is recognized, one cannot be sure that the total expenditures are too large, or that we would be better off with a ceiling on the total, unless better ways were found for deciding how the total should be distributed.

The case for a constitutional amendment, at least in the minds of many of its supporters, is derived more from the fear of excessive expenditures than of excessive deficits. In fact, the basic position of some proponents is that the growth of government is *the* great threat to a free society. I take that to be the position of Milton Friedman. It seems to me exaggerated, for reasons explained below.

Even for the concerns that motivate it, however, the constitutional amendment would not be an adequate solution. Every version of the amendment allows the limitations on deficits and on spending to be overridden by two-thirds of the Congress. Also, as is widely acknowledged, the limitations can be evaded by loan guarantees, regulations, and other ways of affecting the use of the national output that do not appear in this budget. Moreover, the amendment would do nothing about the composition of both the expenditure and the revenue sides of the budget, which are in some respects as important as the total level of expenditures or the deficit.

In other words, the constitutional amendment would not relieve us of the need to learn how to make better decisions about the budget, but would only temporarily conceal the need to do so.

Do Expenditures Rise to Equal Revenues?

The proposition that governments will spend all the revenue they have seems to have been influential with a number of people, including, notably, Ronald Reagan. (This proposition is known as Parkinson's Law.) Several attempts have been made to test the proposition econometrically with, as usual, inconclusive results.

Commonsense observation indicates that the law cannot be taken as an inescapable limit on policy. In its simplest version, the law says that governments will spend what they have. But our experience has been that governments spend all the revenue they have plus more—that is, they run deficits—and the amount of the deficit has not been constant. In other words, the amount of expenditures is determined not only by the amount of revenue but also by prevailing ideas of the proper (or tolerable) size of deficits. These ideas change, and have been changed by experience as well as argument. Whether a revenue increase will be matched by an expenditure increase can be influenced by these ideas.

The applicability of Parkinson's Law depends on the reasons for the revenue increase. A revenue increase that occurs spontaneously, perhaps as a result of economic growth and inflation, is more likely to be spent than a revenue increase that is legislated in an effort to reduce the deficit. The two kinds of revenue increases would occur in quite different "attitude" environments. Our experience is mainly with the former kind, from which one cannot calculate the result of revenue increases of the second kind.

In fact, our experience does not indicate that even the kind of revenue increase that occurs spontaneously or accidentally is spent in its entirety. The revenue increases that came with World War II, the Korean War, and the Vietnam War were followed by tax rate reductions. They may have resulted in higher expenditures than would have resulted if taxes were not raised during the war, but certainly not by the amount of the revenue increase. Similarly, the revenue increase—fiscal dividend, as it was called—that came with economic growth and inflation from 1955 to 1980 was not entirely spent. Much of it was returned to taxpayers through rate reduction. Essentially, all of the increase in real revenues that resulted from the impact of inflation and growth on a progressive, unindexed tax system was returned in rate reduction (excluding Social Security taxes).

In any case, even if the evidence were clear—which it is not—that in the past all revenue increases had been spent, that would still not be conclusive for policy in the future. Obviously there would be no point to *policy* research if it were assumed that all past experience would inevitably be repeated. The object is to discover how things can be improved—that is, changed.

Existing procedures probably do contain a bias in the revenue-expenditure relation. It is likely that some expenditures will be made if the revenue is available without a legislated tax increase that would not be made if a tax increase were required. Whether the bias is in the direction of too much spending or too little cannot be said *a priori*. Unwillingness to spend if a tax increase is required may be excessive, or willingness to spend if no tax increase is required may be excessive. Inertia operates in both directions—reluctance to raise taxes and weak incentives to cut them. We should be looking for ways to reduce this bias—in whichever direction it works.

Are Government Expenditures Harmful Per Se?

Much discussion of the budget today proceeds on the assumptions, usually implicit, that government spending is a bad thing and any process that will reduce government spending is a good thing. Probably no one literally believes that. But there is an assumption that any reduction from the present level of spending would be a good thing, although it is unclear how we know that $1 trillion of expenditures, or about 25 percent of GNP, is too much if we don't know that zero would be best, and no one is suggesting that government expenditures be reduced to zero. If, then, there is some optimum level of spending that is not zero, how do we know that it isn't 25 percent of GNP, or 50 percent?

Of course, in a certain sense expenditure, which is the cost of something, is a bad thing. It is always better to have less cost if it can be reduced without reducing the end product. It would be good to spend less for defense if we could have just as much defense for less expenditure. There are certainly areas in which we could have just as much of some government product with less expenditure, but those cases would have to be found, not be assumed *a priori* to exist. There are probably also cases in which a government product is not worth its cost—a subjective evaluation—but that simply cannot be assumed to be true for all government expenditures. Everyone would recognize that some government expenditures, by his standards, yield a worthwhile product. Similarly, he must also recognize that other expenditures yield worthwhile products by someone else's standards. Once said, there is room for discussion, argument, and the exercise of political power, but not for the assertion of objective laws about the excessive character of government spending *per se*.

Assertion of a general proposition about the evil of government spending in the aggregate, as distinguished from arguments about the value of particular expenditures, usually rests upon one or both of two propositions. The first is that a high level of government spending retards economic growth. The second is that a high level of government spending is a threat to individual freedom.

There are two things to say about government spending and

economic growth. The first is that growth isn't everything. There are objectives of government expenditures that are more important than the growth that may be sacrificed to get them. The second is that the connection between government spending and economic growth is not at all clear. The U.S. economy grew almost exactly as fast in the forty high-expenditure years 1948-88 as in the forty low-expenditure years 1889-1929, excluding the depression and war years. Many government expenditures can be viewed as contributing to economic growth. For example, nothing could be more damaging to the growth of the U.S. economy than to be overrun by the Soviets or to wage war with them. The U.S. defense program can thus be chalked up as making a positive contribution to growth. Other expenditures may have an adverse effect on growth, but then we are dealing with those particulars, not with expenditures *per se*.

It is of course true that an increase in government expenditures reduces the freedom of individuals to spend their own incomes. Yet individual spending has increased despite the rise of government spending, simply because total spending has increased so much. The real concern about spending and freedom is about political freedom, presumably about the power the expenditure gives to government to reward or punish people by granting or withholding benefits. But the expenditure for interest payments and the "entitlement" payments, like Social Security, made according to an objective formula, gives no such power. And the defense expenditure is on balance an essential for freedom. Surely there are opportunities for corruption and for political use of the spending power. But the threat to freedom seems remote.

In many respects, Americans are freer today than they were in the past century when government expenditures were much lower. There are many countries around the world today where government expenditures are much higher relative to the national incomes than in the United States—Western Europe, for example —but where there seems to be no consequent loss of freedom. Nonetheless, none of this is to assert the proposition that government spending is a good thing. It is only to say that no general statement about government spending in total can be valid.

Is the Relevant Information Obtainable?

The kinds of information that would be required to make good decisions about the budget reveal that we are far from knowing what we would like to know. The list is endless. We do not know:

- Whether deficits reduce national saving, and by how much in relation to the size of the deficit;

- How much a reduction in national saving reduces future economic growth;

- How much any particular tax affects work, saving, investment, and productivity;

- What the military strength and intentions of the Soviet Union are and what amounts of national security we get with what amounts of defense expenditure;

- If the federal government increases expenditures for a certain purpose in a certain way, say $10 billion for Medicare, how much that will increase national—public and private—expenditures for that purpose, in this case medical care, and how much that will help achieve the objective, in this case health.

To say that we need to know such things in order to make good budget decisions would seem both obvious and hopeless. But the fact is that there are budget decisions that cannot be avoided and implicit assumptions that also cannot be avoided. An effort to improve budgetmaking must, therefore, include an effort to improve our knowledge about the unknowns.

There are, however, some hopeful signs.

First, if it were literally true that we knew nothing about the answers to some of these questions, that itself would be useful information. For example, suppose that we did not know at all whether, or in what proportions, an increase in Medicare expenditures would (a) increase the medical services obtained by elderly people, (b) increase the consumption of elderly people for objects other than medical care, (c) increase the incomes of health professionals, and (d) reduce the medical services obtained by nonelderly people. This information about our ignorance would be relevant in deciding whether to make an expenditure that is justified by its presumed effect on the medical care received by elderly people. One might offer a general precept that if you do not know the effect of what you are doing, you should stop doing it if that is possible, which is not always the case.

Second, we do in fact have more information than we are using about some things, even if it is less than we would like. Common discussion of the effects of budget deficits, for example, ranges from—or alternates between—unbelievably small effects and unbelievably large effects. Similarly, discussion and decisions about taxes frequently imply magnitudes of effects that are outside of the range of all supportable estimates. If the right questions are asked, the possibility of answers that rest upon wild assumptions or superstitions is greatly reduced.

Third, in general, uncertainty about the validity of the information relevant to decisions calls for making only gradual changes in policy, so that the consequences of the changes can be observed. The suggestion of this book, therefore, is not for a radical transformation of the budget in response to uncertain information, but for cautious changes that could be guided by more relevant information than is now employed, even if the new information is imperfect.

Fourth, and probably most important, if the right questions are asked in the right way (i.e., if their real connection with real decisions becomes more apparent), then greater effort will be directed to finding better answers. The government of the United States is inescapably involved in significantly influencing the behavior of a large and complex economy. It can afford to devote more resources to learning how to do that better.

If information on the relation of budget policies to the allocation of the national output, and through that to various national objectives, became an important ingredient in making decisions, clearly those people who have an interest in one policy or another will try to produce information to support their interests. No budgetary process is going to eliminate that. But to focus the argument on the allocation of the national output will reduce the opportunity for deception. It will promote reliance on quantifiable propositions rather than emotional appeal to symbols like "the balanced budget" or "no tax increase." It will call attention to consequences of policy that are not visible in the budget itself. It will reduce the opportunity for evasion by subsidies, guarantees, and regulations that affect the use of the national output but appear in the budget only partially if at all.

In the end, we have to rely on competition in the production of information. If the information were to be generated entirely by the president and his staff, one could not have much confidence that the new information would change the outcome very much. The opportunities for manipulating information, if one has a monopoly on it, are great. We have to count on congressional forces with competing interests to provide a check on the information coming from the administration. Even more, we have to count on private groups with divergent interests, possibly with no interest other than to set limits to the political and partisan misuse of information.

Do Budget Deficits Reduce National Saving?

It is a basic proposition of this book that the decision about the size of the deficit or surplus is like the decision about how much to spend for defense, or for Aid to Families with Dependent Children, or other decisions about the budget. That is, it is a decision that has certain effects on the allocation of the national output, and the decision should be made with reference to the desirability of those specific effects, not with reference to some traditional or intuitive rule. The decision to have a deficit equal to 4 percent of GNP is like the decision to spend 6 percent of the GNP on defense. Either decision may be wise or unwise, but there is no more reason to think, *a priori*, that the proper size of the deficit is zero than that the proper size of the defense program is 3 percent of GNP. Either might be true, but it would have to be supported by evidence in particular situations.

The assumption used in this book is that the size of the deficit, or surplus, has an effect on the size of national saving and therefore on the size of national investment, and that this effect should be taken into account in deciding on the size of the surplus or deficit. This assumption is not, however, critical to the basic proposal put forth here—namely, that we should think about the effects of the deficit or surplus on the allocation of the national output (rather than on savings and investment). If the deficit or surplus did not affect the national output in the way assumed here, it would still be desirable to base decisions on whatever other effects there actually were.

Nonetheless, the assumption that deficits reduce national saving and investment deserves some attention. Until recently there would have been a general agreement among economists on the validity of this assumption (except for a Keynesian qualification under some conditions). The standard view was that the deficit had to be financed out of private savings, so that the total saving available to support private investment and contribute to economic growth would be reduced. This was the real content of the proposition that government deficits are a burden on future generations and also the reason for tolerating deficits to finance government productive investment, which would offset the loss of private investment.

The Keynesian qualification relates to the condition in which the economy was operating below its potential, or below full employment. In that case a budget deficit would reduce the nation's *propensity to save*—that is, the proportion of the national income that would be saved—but not necessarily the *actual* amount of saving. The reduction of the propensity to save will make the actual level of national income higher, and even though the proportion actually saved is lower, the dollar amount saved, and invested, is higher because the national income is higher.

In the past dozen years, since the publication of Robert Barro's article "Are Government Bonds Net Wealth?" in 1974,[1] these views have been increasingly challenged. This challenge goes under the name "Ricardian Equivalence Theory," after the British economist who suggested the possibility 150 years ago but did not believe it was true. The argument is that when the government incurs a deficit, taxpayers incur an obligation to service the debt through taxes. If the deficit results from a cut in current taxes, the taxpayers' net after-tax income position is unaffected; the increase in current after-tax income is offset by the decline in the present value of future after-tax income. Since their after-tax income position, or true net wealth, is unaffected, they will not change their consumption or savings behavior. Since their current after-tax income is increased, they will seem to save more, but that apparent increase will be balanced by the unmeasured increase in their liabilities. Total national saving, public and private, will be unaffected, and there will be no crowding out of private investment.

This is a plausible theory of private behavior, on certain assumptions—that people foresee the future tax liabilities implicit in the current deficit, that they consider all of these future tax liabilities as a subtraction from their wealth (which implies, among other things, that they value their heirs as themselves), and that their current consumption is governed by their wealth, including the present value of their future after-tax income, and is not constrained by current access to liquidity. Clearly, these conditions are never fully met, but they may be met in part for some people. So the significance of the theory depends on the extent to which people actually behave as postulated, a question that can only be answered by empirical observation.

Unfortunately there have been very few cases in American history that can provide tests of the theory. Aside from recessions and wars, before 1980 deficits were so small relative to the GNP that their effects on saving were drowned out by other factors. The largest deficits we ever had, relative to GNP (at least in the period of modern statistics), were in World War II. At that time, private savings increased, but that could be explained by rationing and by patriotic appeals to save. Even so, the rise of private saving did not offset the rising deficits, and private investment declined.

The one big test we have of the Barro theory in the United States is the deficits of the years 1982-87. Although there are some arguments about the definition and measurement of saving, one can certainly not find support for the theory in that experience. By standard measurements, consumption was high and private saving was low during the period of exceptionally large deficits. But that was only one case, and there may have been forces at work to nullify the prediction of the Barro theory that private saving would rise. Indeed, some studies suggest that the theory has stood up in other countries. We do not seem to be capable of any general and confident statement about whether or to what degree or under what circumstances the theory may be valid.

Despite this uncertainty, it seems prudent to base policy on the premises that deficits are a subtraction from national saving, and that when the economy is at high employment deficits crowd out private investment. This situation might change if we lived with very large deficits—even larger than the recent ones—for a long time. Consciousness of the implications for future taxation might rise, and people might behave more like the far-seeing calculators of Barro's theory. That would be especially likely if the crowding out of private investment came noticeably to diminish the prospects for future incomes, so that people would feel impelled to save for their own futures and those of their children.

The Barro theory does not maintain that spending and not spending are equivalent. That is, it does not deny that an increase in government expenditures will crowd out private spending, but only that this crowding out will not depend on whether the government expenditures are financed by taxing or borrowing. Moreover, there is no presumption that an increase in government expenditure will crowd out private investment rather than private consumption.

The Barro theory does, however, have implications for the expenditure side of the budget, especially on the future implications of today's budget decisions. How is the present behavior of private parties influenced by the knowledge that they (or their heirs) will be beneficiaries of future expenditures? The leading case is Social Security. The government established a program that promises to pay benefits in the future. How will the anticipation of these future benefits affect behavior today? Will the prospective beneficiaries consume more during their working lives because they can look forward to a pension from the government? This seems more plausible than that people will save more in anticipation of future taxes, because individuals seem to be more conscious of their Social Security benefits than of future taxes. There is also more empirical evidence of the negative effect of future benefits on private saving than of the positive effect of future taxes, although estimates of the size of the negative effect of future benefits are much in dispute.

Other budgetary decisions may affect the rate of national saving. These include decisions about the tax structure and about government capital expenditures. Where these effects on national saving seem consequential they should be taken into account when decisions are made, for example, on the effect of deficits on national saving. There is no objective, mechanical rule for making these decisions. The relation between decision and outcome—be it national saving or national security or national health—is uncertain, and the value placed on these and other objectives is a matter of judgment to be settled, in the end, by the political process. All one can urge is that the connections be estimated as well as possible, and that the judgment be as explicit as possible. On the basis of present evidence, these estimates should not start with the Barro assumption that the effect of deficits will be offset by private saving.

International Consequences of Budget Deficits

It is important to distinguish between investment in the United States and investment owned by Americans. The savings of Americans are equal to the investments owned by Americans. That may be greater or smaller than the investment in the United States. The savings of Americans are equal to investment in the United States plus net investment of Americans abroad, which is the net outflow of capital from the United States, or minus net investment of foreigners here, which is the net inflow of capital from abroad.

If the federal budget deficit reduces total national saving—public plus private—it will reduce investment owned by Americans. That reduction may be divided between investment in the United States and investment abroad. How it is divided will depend on the relative attractiveness—to foreigners as well as Americans—of those investments. If foreigners and Americans invest here, there will be a net inflow of funds, and investment in the United States will exceed investment owned by Americans.

During the 1980s, a large part of the crowding out caused by the federal budget deficit took the form of a crowding out of American investment abroad, but only a small part of it led to reduced investment in the United States. There were several reasons for that. Changes in taxes and some other policies increased the attractiveness of investment here. Economic stagnation in Western Europe and the inability of many less-developed countries to meet their debt obligations reduced the attractiveness of investments outside the United States. Liberalization of capital movements out of Japan opened up a large flow of funds to America. From 1981 to 1987, gross private domestic investment in the United States was 15.9 percent of the GNP. The capital inflow was 1.8 percent of GNP, and the gross investment owned by Americans was 14.1 percent.

(It should be understood that the inflow figures are net of outflows. Also, they say nothing about the form of either the domestic or the foreign investment. Thus, if $500 billion of plant and equipment is built in America, and all of it is owned by Americans but foreigners acquire $100 billion of U.S. government securities, the gross investment owned by Americans is $400 billion. The argument is sometimes heard that the capital inflow did not contribute to investment in the United States, since it was placed in government securities. But Americans would have had to buy the government securities if foreigners had not bought them, and the amount of investment in the United States would have been lower. So foreigners indirectly financed the real investment and acquired a claim to its earnings. The future income earned by the investment financed by foreigners will belong to the foreigners, not to Americans. But Americans have not lost that income, because the income would not have been produced if the foreigners had not made the investment here. We lost the income when we ran the budget deficits.)

The fact that the crowding out took the form it did, allowing investment in America to continue with little diminution, did not insulate the United States from the effects of the deficit. But it did have some distributional consequences. The capital inflow was matched by a reduction in the U.S. trade balance, which injured U.S. exporting and import-competing industries. That was, of course, much noticed during the 1980s. Less noticed was the fact that the capital inflow assisted U.S. capital-using industries, such as housing. It also affected the distribution of income between labor and capital in the United States as well as abroad. In the United States, the fact that capital was available when the budget deficit rose to high levels held down the returns to U.S. savers below what they would otherwise have received, but it kept the wages of American workers from being injured by a decline in the amount of productive capital they worked with. The reverse happened in the countries from which the capital came to the United States.

Whether these distributional shifts, among industries and between capital and labor, should be a concern of public policy is an open question. Does the fact that a budget deficit causes a trade deficit make it more important to avoid budget deficits than it would otherwise be? The common answer to that seems to be affirmative, but the case is not at all clear. There are gainers as well as losers within the American economy, and there is no obvious reason why the government should be concerned with that particular redistribution. The argument is sometimes made that the crowding out financed by a capital inflow and trade deficit is particularly unstable and threatens disruption of the economy if foreigners were to decide that they no longer want to invest in America. But the same disruption could occur if Americans decide that they no longer want to invest in America, either because they think that the budget deficit threatens inflation or for some other reason.

Because a large budget deficit in a large country has important effects on other countries, the size of the U.S. and other nations' budget deficits has become the subject of international discussion and efforts at coordination among governments. The mere fact that other countries are affected does not establish a need for coordination, however. The low savings propensities of private Americans affect other countries and the international flow of capital, but are not considered to require international coordination. The situation is no different if the low savings propensities of Americans are expressed through a decision to run a budget deficit. If the international consequences of our budget deficits or surpluses are considered to be a reason for special concern, despite the negative opinion given here, this concern can be incorporated in the budget process.

The concern about the international consequences of the budget deficit is similar to the concern expressed in the early 1970s about the effect of budget deficits on residential construction. The typical financing of residential construction resulted in the brunt of crowding out being borne by the housing industry, since the thrifts could not attract funds when interest rates rose due to a ceiling on the interest they could pay on deposits. This differential effect on housing seemed to be another reason to avoid deficits. (It was a reason, naturally, that appealed especially to the secretary of housing and urban development.) But the reason disappeared when that particular imperfection in the capital markets was corrected.

Limits to Deficits and Debt

The suggestion that the size of the deficit or surplus should be chosen as a means of affecting the rate of private investment and thereby the rate of economic growth raises the question whether there are any limits to this choice. More pointedly, can deficits go on "forever"?

Consideration of effects on private investment does indicate some limits to the size of the surplus or deficit. There used to be a view among economists (the "stagnationist" thesis in vogue about fifty years ago) that the economy could not function if the surplus was too large, and there was in fact some concern that it would become too large. The fear was that investment opportunities would be inadequate for the savings the surplus would represent, and as a result total demand would be inadequate to keep the economy operating at high employment. In terms of the argument of this book, the condition can be described as one in which the abundance of capital drives the rate of return to capital down to zero, so that a policy of generating savings by running a surplus makes no sense. Whether that is even a theoretical possibility need not detain us here. It is surely not a present or realistically foreseeable condition. In any case, a reasonable appraisal of the value of running a surplus in order to generate savings would take account of the probable rate of return on investment.

Consideration of the effect on savings and the capital stock sets a limit in the other direction on the size of the deficit. If the deficit exceeds net private saving, there will be negative net investment. Capital depreciation will not be offset, and the capital stock will decline. If this continues, in time the capital stock will be exhausted, and it will be impossible to run a deficit in excess of net private saving. Presumably, the need to reduce the deficit would be recognized before this point is reached.

Consideration of the effects of surpluses or deficits on savings, investment, and growth therefore does set limits to their size. The question is whether any limit is set by other considerations.

It is often heard that deficits cannot go on forever. That is not literally correct, however. A deficit of a size that does not raise the ratio of the debt to the GNP can go on forever—which is not to say that it is wise. For example, the federal debt held by the public is now about 40 percent of the GNP. If the GNP grows by 6 percent a year (in nominal terms) the debt can also grow by 6 percent a year without raising the ratio of debt to GNP. That would permit a deficit equal to 2.4 percent of GNP. Then, if interest rates are stable, the ratio of federal interest payments to GNP would also be stable. And if the deficit or surplus in the budget excluding interest is stable as a fraction of GNP, the ratio of the total deficit to the GNP will be stable. This combination of conditions could go on forever—at least as far as the arithmetic is concerned.

What cannot go on forever is a rise in the ratio of the debt and the interest burden to GNP. This is, of course, a characteristic that the debt and the interest burden share with a number of other variables. For example, it has been observed that the cost of a military airplane has been rising much faster than the GNP for a long time. If this continues, the cost of a single airplane could exceed the whole GNP. This is an interesting observation, but not yet a cause for alarm.

One can specify various conditions under which the deficit would cause an endless rise in the ratio of debt and interest burden to the GNP. For example, one might assume that government revenues equal expenditures for all purposes other than interest, so that its deficit is equal to the interest burden. If the interest rate is higher than the growth rate of the economy, the debt will rise faster than the GNP and the debt-to-GNP ratio will rise endlessly.

This rise in the debt-to-GNP ratio cannot go on forever, because at some point the deficit will exceed private saving and will not be financeable. That is, the limit is the same that is emphasized throughout this book, namely, concern for savings, investment, and the stock of capital.

There is a certain value in thinking about conditions that cannot go on forever. It indicates the danger of becoming irrevocably committed to a course of action that may be benign at first, but would eventually become extremely harmful. The deficit and the debt are not the only examples; "entitlement" programs, such as Social Security, involve a similar danger. This is not an argument against commitments, but against commitments entered without forethought. The fact that the ratios of debt, deficits, and interest payments to GNP cannot go on rising forever does not mean that they cannot safely, and even desirably, increase for some period of time.

But if these ratios are allowed to increase, there should be some assurance that they are not going to increase endlessly. There should be some understanding of the conditions that would justify an increase as well as of the conditions under which the increase would end. If not, private investors may take the fact of rising ratios as a signal of further rises whose end cannot be foreseen and anticipate future increases of interest rates, inflation, or taxes, with undesirable immediate consequences for investment and the price level.

War is now commonly understood as a condition for temporarily increasing these ratios, one that does not portend an endless increase; indeed, a subsequent reduction in these ratios, as happened after World War II, would probably be the common expectation. Recession is now also understood as a condition in which a rise in the ratios does not foretell an endless rise. In the 1980s these ratios increased, partly but not entirely in connection with a recession, causing some worry but no firm expectation of an explosive increase in the future. The debt-to-GNP and interest-to-GNP ratios then started from unusually low levels.

Recognition of the dangerous consequences of allowing the debt and deficit to rise endlessly as a fraction of the GNP emphasizes the imperative for reasonable prudence and foresight in the conduct of budget policy. The same can be said about the dangerous consequences of allowing the defense budget to decline endlessly or the state of national literacy to deteriorate. There is no substitute for good sense in the management of any aspect of the budget. The hope of this book is that the possibility of good sense will be increased if decisionmakers can be brought to look more realistically at the consequences of their actions.

How Should the Budget, and the Surplus or Deficit, Be Measured?

There is no single proper measurement of the budget. The appropriate measurement depends on the purpose for which the measurement is being made. The usual, often implicit, notion is that the budget is to be balanced and, if it is balanced, some desired result will be achieved. The proper definition of the budget will then depend upon the results that are sought from balancing. Several different desired results can be imagined, each calling for a different definition of the budget. For example:

• To make the budget's drain upon national savings zero, or constant, the outgo side of the budget could be defined to exclude capital expenditure.

• To hold constant the budget's effect on aggregate demand, the budget could be defined to include only expenditures and receipts that enter into private incomes (like the "national income accounts" budget calculated by the Department of Commerce) excluding all transactions in existing assets.

• If the object is to "discipline" the government, expenditures should be defined as broadly as possible and the revenues as narrowly as possible.

• If the object is to stabilize tax rates over time, expenditure should be defined as the average of future expected expenditure levels (relative to the tax base), or the present value of future expenditures should be compared with the present value of future revenues at present rates.

• Other purposes can be imagined, such as controlling the government's draft on capital markets, understood to be something other than the supply of savings.

Even if the purpose of calculating the budget is specified, there is no precise, feasible definition. Defining the budget means deciding that some transactions count, from the standpoint of the purpose, and some do not. But the included transactions will not be homogeneous, and will not count equally. For example, if the intent is to measure the contribution (positive or negative) to the nation's capital stock, it will be seen that different expenditures are "consumption" in immeasurably different degrees. Similarly, different revenues will be "consumption-restraining" in immeasurably different degrees. Drawing a line between transactions that are included and those that are excluded is to some degree arbitrary, leading to the logical but impractical suggestion that each transaction be assigned a weight from 0 to 1, representing its relative impact on the object the budget is supposed to measure. Thus, if the object is national investment, expenditure on roads might get a weight of 1, education 0.5, health 0.3, and so on. But if the object is effect on aggregate demand, purchases of newly produced goods and services might get a weight of 1, transfer payments 0.5, interest payments 0.2, income tax –0.9, sale of bonds –0.2, and so on. But of course we do not know the proper weights, and weights would differ for different purposes.

So there is no simple definition of the budget that is consistently relevant or precisely accurate for any one purpose. Still we need a definition. Conceptually, we could dispense with defining the budget and say that we will continuously monitor all of the transactions separately, appraising their significance for the objects of policy and being continually prepared to revise the decision about any transaction. Practically, we cannot do that. It would be too expensive, too time consuming, too disturbing to the government and the private sector, and would require too much information. We need some budget to serve as a standard or rule of policy to be followed during a period when some things but not everything should be kept stable—not forever but for some period.

In the view expressed here, there is no reason for the budget, however defined, to have a zero balance at any time or for the size of the surplus or deficit to be constant over any long period of time. However the budget is defined, the size of the surplus or deficit should be decided on the basis of the desired effect on the rate of national investment. In making such a decision, account would be taken of the amount of investment incorporated in the expenditure side of the budget, the rate of private saving, and the expected future national commitments (such as those implicit in the Social Security program). From this standpoint it would not matter how the government budget is defined, because the accounts we are looking at are not the government budget accounts but the national accounts. Moreover, the budget position decided in this way would not be a constant but would respond to changes in the private saving rate, the actual and expected economic growth rate, and similar factors.

Nevertheless, there is a need to promote the short-run stability of the economy, to keep the budget position reasonably stable from year to year, as will be discussed in Part II. That is, large variations in the budget position that would disturb the economy should be avoided. "Budget position" means, in this connection, the net effect of the budget on aggregate demand. This effect should not change significantly or unpredictably from year to year, although we should not be much concerned about the *level* of this effect. There is need for a rule of policy so that when the surplus or deficit is constant, the aggregate demand effect of the budget is constant. There is no available definition of the budget that will meet this test precisely. The best approximation is probably the budget as measured in the national income accounts as it would be at some standard position of the economy. (This standard position has in the past been commonly identified as "high employment," a matter that will be discussed in Part II.)

Thus, we have two different interests in the definition of the budget, which might be reconciled as follows:

a. Decide every five years on the level of the surplus or deficit that it would achieve for each of the next five years in the "aggregate demand" budget.

b. Decide that level on the basis of the desirable contribution of the budget to net national saving—a decision that would be a matter of social choice.

The expected future level of government expenditures is relevant for deciding on the present surplus or deficit. The higher the expected future government expenditures, the higher the present surplus should be—other things being equal—in order to avoid the need for excessive tax rates later on (on the principle that tax rates of 20 percent for ten years followed by 30 percent for ten years have more distorting effects than 25 percent for twenty years), by helping to provide a higher future national income out of which to meet anticipated expenditures.

Unfortunately we do not foresee most expenditures very well, and probably the best we can do for most of the budget is to project a constant ratio to GNP. But we can quite clearly foresee a substantial rise in the ratio of Social Security and Medicare expenditures to GNP. Also, national policy calls for financing these expenditures from a dedicated tax—the payroll tax. These two considerations argue for putting Social Security and Medicare outside "The Budget" in a separate account. Under present arrangements, this account will be running a "surplus" (over current benefits but not over accruing liabilities) for the next twenty-five years or so. Putting the account outside the budget will not answer the question of the proper size of the deficit or surplus in the rest of the budget and therefore in the consolidated budget. It may, however, serve as a crude reminder of the obligations that are being accrued, and that should be taken into account when deciding on the size of the consolidated surplus or deficit.

Does Cutting Taxes Raise Revenue?

The idea that reducing tax rates increases the revenue, and vice versa, had a considerable vogue beginning in 1978 or 1979 and lasting, I suppose, until about 1984. That idea was supposed to have been derived from the "Laffer Curve," although the curve provided no evidence that the idea applied to the United States in the twentieth century or at any other time. The idea has now been generally discredited, and even people who once seemed to believe it now deny that they ever did. However, there still are remnants of the idea around, and it is worth examining briefly.

The logic of the Laffer Curve is that no revenue will be raised if the tax rate is zero, no revenue will be raised if the tax rate is 100 percent, but some revenue will be raised at some rates—not necessarily all rates—between zero and 100 percent. (The proposition that there will be no revenue at a tax rate of 100 percent applies to taxes on income, because people will presumably not undertake activity that yields income if they get nothing, after tax, for it. It may not apply to other kinds of taxes. Probably a tax of 100 percent on cigarettes would yield some income, although there is probably some higher tax rate on cigarettes that would not yield any income.) The Laffer Curve shows that some tax increases would raise the revenue and some tax increases would reduce the revenue. An increase in the rate from zero to some positive number (less than 100 percent) would raise it; an increase from some lower number to 100 percent would reduce it. That is all we can tell from the Laffer Curve.

The operational question is where we stand on the Laffer Curve. Are we on the part of the curve where a tax increase raises the revenue or where it reduces the revenue? The answer depends on the *ratio* of the percent change in the tax rate to the percent change in the tax base. Only if the percent reduction in the tax base is larger than the percent increase in the tax rate will an increase of the tax rate reduce the revenue. Thus, suppose that the tax base is income. A tax rate of 20 percent on an income of $100 billion will yield $20 billion of revenue. If an increase of the tax rate to, say, 22 percent reduced the income to $95 billion, the revenue would rise to $20.9 billion. Only if income fell below $90.9 billion would the revenue be reduced by the tax increase. Merely to say that the tax increase will reduce income is not enough to demonstrate that a tax increase will reduce the revenue.

Much work has gone into studying whether the U.S. tax system is now or has recently been in a position in which a reduction of rates would raise the revenue and an increase of rates would reduce the revenue. With one exception the evidence is strongly negative. Nothing we know about the response of the supply of labor or of savings to income tax rates supports the idea that an increase of rates would reduce the supply of either labor or savings enough to reduce the revenue. The exception is the case of the taxation of capital gains, where there is some evidence that a reduction of tax rates increases the realization of gains enough to raise the revenue. The question here is whether this phenomenon is only a change in the timing of realizations, so that while there may be a surge of revenue, that is essentially an advance of revenue that would have been collected anyway. It should be noted that the capital gains tax has the peculiar feature that if realization is postponed long enough, the tax may be escaped entirely because capital gains are canceled at the death of the holder. That makes decisions about realization more sensitive to the tax rate than they would be if the tax would eventually have to be paid. All that can be confidently said is that studies leave much uncertainty about whether or not a reduction of the capital gains tax would raise the revenue. But no one can think that the increased revenue from that source could be substantial in relation to a $1 trillion budget.

The fact that revenues have increased since the Reagan administration tax reduction of 1981 is sometimes cited as evidence for the claim that tax reduction increases the revenue. Of course, the basic fact is that in a growing economy with some inflation revenues will rise from year to year if tax rates are held constant. Revenues almost always rise in the United States. The question is whether revenues have risen abnormally fast, or faster than they would otherwise have done, since the 1981 tax cut. The answer to that is negative. Revenues from 1981 to 1988 have risen exceptionally slowly, in real terms, not exceptionally rapidly. Revenues other than the revenues from the Social Security taxes, which were raised, have risen especially slowly.

One should expect that the relation between tax changes and revenue changes would vary with differences in the character and rate of taxation. For example, cutting a 50 percent income tax rate by 10 percent, to 45 percent, should result in a larger percentage gain in income and a smaller percentage loss of revenue than cutting a 20 percent rate by 10 percent to 18 percent. Cutting the 50 percent rate to 45 percent raises after-tax income 10 percent, from 50 percent to 55 percent. Cutting the 20 percent rate to 18 percent raises after-tax income by 2.5 percent, from 80 percent to 82 percent. Possibly there are some cases in the United States system where a reduction of taxes would raise the revenue, but there is no reason to think that such cases are common or that any significant addition to the revenue could be obtained by reducing tax rates. Similarly, there is no reason to think that revenue cannot be increased by raising tax rates, although the percentage increase in the revenue may not be—probably will not be—as large as the percentage increase in the rates.

· 4 ·
Reforming the
Budgeting Process

$\mathbf{R}$eform of the federal budget requires focusing the attention of decisionmakers—the president, the Congress, and ultimately the public—on the real consequences of their budget decisions. These real consequences concern the allocation of the national output and ultimately the achievement of important national objectives. Budget decisions influence how much of the national output is devoted to investment, how much to medical care, how much to military force, and so on. These allocations are important because they affect the rate of economic growth (or, more specifically, the incomes of our children and grandchildren), the health of the population, national security, and so on.

Our general failure to think about the budget in this way, and the imperative need to do so, is highlighted by the way we "think" about the budget deficit. A reduction in the budget deficit is now almost universally accepted as essential, and there is almost universal dissatisfaction with the pace at which that is being achieved. But if one asks why the deficit should be reduced, no convincing answers are ever forthcoming. This raises two possibilities. One is that there is no good reason to reduce the budget deficit. The other is that although there is a good reason, decisionmakers are not impressed by it.

The budget deficit acquires meaning if one can say that it affects the allocation of the national output in specific ways—that it reduces the supply of national saving (perhaps not dollar for dollar; that is a matter to be examined) and thus reduces the share of the national output that is invested. Having said that, one can then argue about whether one wants that effect on investment, and about what consequences a change in investment would have. The most important of these consequences is an effect on the future growth of national income. (The size of this effect is also something to consider.) But when we get to the point of considering the effect of the budget policy on the future level of national income, we have reached a magnitude that we can have a feeling about and value in a way that we cannot value the size of the budget deficit.

To have a feeling about the future level of national income is meaningful only in a comparative sense. Most people would agree that a higher level of future national income is a good thing. That answers no questions. The issue is what we would be willing to sacrifice in order to increase future national income. It is only meaningful, in an operational sense, to say that we want more future national income if we are also saying that we want it more than something else, which we are willing to give up to get it.

A decision to reduce the budget deficit in order to increase national saving, in order to devote more of the national output to investment, and in order to have more future national income, is a decision to devote less of the national output to something else. That is not the same as saying that some other government expenditures must be reduced or that some taxes must be raised. These are not the costs of devoting more of the national output to investment; they are the means by which that cost is accepted or imposed. The additional investment must come not out of the budget but out of the total uses of national income, including both private and governmental uses. To say that the deficit should be reduced in order to increase investment is to say that we would rather decrease some other use of the national income—it implies a comparison.

Reducing the deficit in order to increase investment is used here only as an example. The same point could be illustrated by a decision, say, to increase the share of the national output going to the defense program in order to increase national security. This implies a decision that increasing the share of defense is sufficiently important to justify decreasing some other use of the national income—whether public—like education—or private—like consumption.

What this means, then, is that what is being budgeted is not the $1 trillion in the government's budget but the nearly $5 trillion in the national income. And what has to be compared is the value of alternative uses of the national income, not of the budget. The significance of this single point, and how commonly it is disregarded, can be seen from the usual consideration of the defense budget. The problem is usually discussed in terms of a trade-off between defense expenditures and other *government* expenditures. In fact, the relevant and realistic trade-off is between defense expenditures and all other uses of the national output.

To say that the government is budgeting the national income implies nothing about the degree of detail involved. Some uses must be budgeted in complete detail—thus, it must decide not only *that* $300 billion should be spent for defense but also *how* it should be spent. Obviously the government cannot, should not, and does not budget the entire national income in anything like that detail. One could imagine a national budget consisting of two parts—a "government" part, which the government allocates totally, and a "private" part, whose total size is influenced by the government budget but not its composition. But in fact the government budget deliberately influences the allocation of output *within* the private sector, and does it in ways that are related to objectives for which the government has some responsibility. The decision about the size of the budget deficit influences how private output is divided between consumption and investment. The decision about the structure of taxes and transfer payments influences the division of private consumption between the poor and the rich. Decisions about tax deductions and loan subsidies influence how much of private spending goes for construction of new houses. Some federal expenditures, as for education and medical care, either induce or reduce nonfederal spending for the same purposes.

Budget decisions should reflect as clear a view as possible of their effects on the allocation of the national output in areas related to objectives for which the government has responsibility. To achieve this will require basic changes in the way the budget is presented, discussed, and acted upon.

The President's Budget

The initial formulation of the budget and its presentation to the Congress and the people are the responsibility of the president. The budget as now written and presented gives little indication of what the president's proposals are intended to accomplish except in the most immediate sense. More or less money is to be spent for this or that program, but what effect that is intended to have on the lives of Americans is rarely made clear.

The budget should be presented in three levels:

1. National objectives

2. Allocation of the national output to further those objectives

3. Programs to achieve that allocation of the national output

The president's budget should be based on an explicit view of what the nation's chief problems and objectives are. Nothing in this proposal restricts the view that the president should have of this. The following statement illustrates what this view might be:

> The United States faces a powerful enemy, whose conventional military forces outstrip ours and threaten our security. The United States is very rich, has the highest per capita income in history. But per capita income is growing slowly, compared to our recent experiences. However rich we are, the loss of the expectation of rapid, visible improvement in living standards removes an invigorating and encouraging aspect of life in America. Also, even though we are on the average very rich a certain, relatively small, number of people

have incomes so low and living conditions so miserable that improvement is a high national priority. Finally, the quality of life in America is worsened, and the survival of a free society itself endangered, by the illiteracy of too many Americans, by their ignorance and their lack of understanding of our society's values. Thus, the nation's most important goals at this time are to strengthen our defenses, to raise the rate of economic growth, to improve the lot of the poorest among us and to elevate the understanding of the population. To say that these are the most important objectives is to say that some other things, although valuable, are less important. The chief among these is to sustain and to advance rapidly the level of consumption of people who are not poor.

Such a position should be based upon and supported by the relevant evidence. In the defense decisionmaking process there is a stage called "net assessment" in which military and intelligence experts try to appraise the security situation of the country and how that situation would be changed by possible changes in the U.S. defense program. The net assessment, which leaves many uncertainties, both about the facts and about policy, is prepared for the use of the president and his top advisers. A similar approach could be used for other national objectives. The process does not relieve the president of the responsibility for exercising his own judgment and expressing his own values. But it would help him to make better decisions and to explain them to the Congress and the public in terms that allow the choices to be evaluated.

The second element in the budget should be a statement of the allocation of the national output that the president believes consistent with or necessary for the achievement of his stated objectives. This could take the form of a description of the present (or recent past) and indications of desired changes. Which categories or classifications should be shown in terms of uses of the national output will depend on the chosen objectives. For example:

National Security (defense and foreign affairs)
Private Investment
Public Investment

Education

Health

Consumption of the Poor (excluding education and health)

Consumption of the Nonpoor (excluding education and health)

Other Public Services

A different set of objectives would call for a different classification of uses. For example, if housing construction were a national objective, it would be shown separately from the investment total shown above.

This procedure does not imply that all objectives can be achieved solely by the devotion of more of the national output to them, or even that the greater fulfillment of some objective requires a greater allocation of the national output. Perhaps national security, or educational achievement, can be increased through greater skill or imagination. Perhaps better management is the solution rather than a larger share of the national output. All that is called for is that the president's budget show the allocations of the national output he thinks are required by his objectives.

"Budgeting the national output" means that an increase in the use of national output for one purpose requires a reduction in the use for another purpose. Constitutional amendments setting a limit to total government expenditures also try to impose this requirement, but the difference is that the choices imposed by the amendment are artificial and not imposed by the facts of life. The limits can be evaded or overturned, usually by little more than a simple majority of Congress. They leave possibilities for evasion by "off-budget" devices, like guarantees, subsidies, regulations, and other means. The limit that total use of output cannot exceed total output is real and cannot be overridden by acts of Congress or evaded by redefinitions.

Some may complain that budgeting the national output will be an invitation to greater government spending than results from present procedures, especially if these procedures were to be constrained by a constitutional amendment. This is possible, but not inevitable. Budgeting the national output means that an increase in government spending in one area is also a reduction of government, or private, spending in another area. This proposal is to make this connection—the real cost—as clear as possible. Whether the government and the public will want to spend more or less when they see the real cost than they otherwise would, no one can say. But the answer to that question is not decisive because the purpose of budget reform is not to reduce government spending or to increase it. It is to get better decisions about the spending.

Budgeting the national output will not eliminate the conventional budget. There will still be need for a "government" budget, with receipts and expenditures, and a deficit or surplus. The estimates of the allocation of the national output will only help explain the *effects* of the budget, making it a useful exercise even if there were a constitutional amendment on the budget. An amendment would only constrain, but not eliminate, the need to decide on total expenditures, total taxes, and the deficit or surplus. These decisions could be made more intelligently if their effects on the broad allocation of the national output were more visible.

Congress and the president cannot, of course, "enact" or manage the allocation of the national output. The government cannot decide that gross private investment should be $375 billion. It can only say that last year investment was $350 billion and therefore it proposes policies—reducing the budget deficit, changing the tax structure, or some other—that it estimates will raise that to $375 billion, which it believes will be good for the country because it will raise future incomes even though it reduces present consumption. The proposal is to go through that step in order to give a more specific and palpable indication of the effects of government decisions.

In fact, the government does not even enact most of the figures that appear in the present budget. It enacts certain tax structures and tax rates, and it largely enacts certain programs that provide for expenditures to be made in certain amounts and under certain conditions. The numbers themselves have not been enacted; they are *estimates* of the receipts, expenditures, and deficits that will result from the decisions made. Thus, Congress did not enact a law requiring that $22 billion be spent on aid to agriculture; it enacted a law specifying that certain amounts would be paid per bushel of wheat, corn, etc., on certain conditions of market prices. It then estimated the total expenditures that law would generate, and that estimate was an important component of the decision to enact it. The proposal here is to introduce another level of estimates—estimates of the allocations of the national output that government programs would generate.

The classification of the national output should conform to the major objectives of national policy as seen by the decisionmakers. The classification will be necessarily much grosser than the classification of budget decisions. That is, the categories of output use will be fewer, bigger, and more general. They must be few enough so that decisionmakers and the public can comprehend them, compare them, and have a judgment about the trade-offs among them. They must not be so large, however, that their contents are too heterogeneous to be meaningful. The illustration above shows eight categories. This number should be accommodated to the decisionmakers' (ultimately the president's) view of the major national objectives, but it should probably not exceed fifteen.

As the federal budget has become larger and more complex, there have been repeated efforts to summarize it and synthesize it so that the president, the Congress, and the public can understand and determine its main directions. The number of budget decisions is in the billions, if the decision of a clerk in the Interior Department to take a new ball-point pen is a decision. If there is to be any control at all, people at higher levels of authority must make more general decisions that constrain the ones below. The budgets presented by the administration and acted upon by Congress probably contain about one thousand decisions on specific expenditure numbers, as well as many other less quantitative decisions. Neither the president nor any member of Congress can balance each of these numbers against all the others. They must make decisions about more summary totals, leaving the division of these totals to subordinates in the administration or specialized committees in the Congress.

For many years the principle of generalization was by organizational unit—so much money for each department and agency, possibly with subdivisions for bureaus within other agencies. But those allocations did not reveal what the money was used for. (FDR used to complain that the agencies were not organized by purpose so that he could not connect the identity of any agency with any outcome. Rexford Tugwell once said that FDR wanted to organize the government by function and would have a Department of Life, with Bureaus of Wild Life, Night Life, and Child Life.)

In 1950 the grouping of expenditures into about twenty functions and seventy-five subfunctions was introduced into the budget document, with the expenditures of various agencies being distributed among the functions and subfunctions. Although appropriations are still made to agencies, the functional division of actual and proposed expenditures is increasingly the basis on which decisions are evaluated and made. The annual Congressional Budget Resolution, for example, intended to set limits to the appropriations that will be subsequently made, is debated and enacted in terms of the functional classifications. In recent years even higher levels of generalization have been used both for exposition and, to some extent, for decisionmaking.

A common classification divides expenditures into only four categories—defense, nondefense discretionary, entitlements and other mandatory spending, and net interest. This is useful for some purposes, but it is a mixture of legal and functional classifications. A more informative effort at aggregation and synthesis was presented in the fiscal 1989 budget (submitted February 1988). The classification was as follows:

National Defense
Net Interest
Payments for Individuals
    Low Income Benefits
    Elderly and Retirees
    Other
Basic Government Functions

Other Administration Priorities
Grants to State and Local Governments
Remaining Programs
Total Outlays
Addendum:
  Health Benefits
  Economic Development and Subsidies

But closer examination reveals how inadequate this classification is to show the effects of the allocations in the budget. The largest part of the expenditures shown are transfers supporting specific private uses of the national output. Thus, the category "Low Income Benefits" is intended to support private use of output by poor people. A complete accounting would also show the effects of the financing side of the budget on the private uses of output. For example, taxes on the poor are an offset to the assistance to the poor. In fact, when discussing the poverty problem the Reagan administration often refers to its cut of taxes for the poor as assistance on a par with direct aid on the expenditure side of the budget. The budget shows, although not included in the above classification, how much expenditure goes for federal investment in physical capital. That is interesting, but its significance can only be appraised alongside an estimate of the budget's effect on private investment, through government borrowing or otherwise. Also, the information in the budget gives no clue to the indirect effects of its expenditures on nonfederal spending. Thus, if we see that federal spending on health has increased from 1.2 percent to 2.7 percent of GNP between 1970 and 1987, we do not know how far this is substituting for private expenditure or how far it is stimulating even more private expenditure.

Aside from its expenditures on defense, by far the largest part of what the federal budget does is influence nonfederal—private, state, and local—uses of national output. It does this through transfer payments, taxes, borrowing, subsidies, and expenditures that are either complementary with or competitive with nonfederal spending. The real consequences of these decisions cannot be appraised until the effects on nonfederal uses of output are seen.

Of course, the gross classification of the uses of the national output suggested here cannot lead directly to specific decisions. To say that we want to spend $300 billion on defense does not tell whether we should build an MX or Midgetman missile. To say that we want to increase the consumption levels of poor people does not tell whether we should increase Aid to Families with Dependent Children or raise the individual income tax exemption. But these individual decisions will be better made if they are brought into conformity with higher-level decisions—about the deficit, defense, taxes (considered as a unit), transfer payments, and "all other." To proceed intelligently, it must be seen that less deficit stands for more private investment, more taxes stands for less private consumption of middle- and upper-income America, some transfer payments stand for the consumption of the very poor, some of the "all other" category stands for productive investment. Until we make such translations, the debate about deficits, taxes, etc., will be largely an appeal to competing shibboleths.

The proposal to budget the national output raises statistical and analytical questions. We do not now have a "functional" classification of the GNP along the lines suggested here, although most of it can be approximated with existing data. Our GNP accounts do not show government investment expenditures separately, although there are estimates of them. If "Education" is to be identified as a separate use, it will be necessary to decide how much investment (public and private) is for education. It will also be necessary to decide which expenditures of the Defense Department, as for ROTC, should be considered education and how to classify the training expenditures within business. Existing statistics do not separate out the "Consumption of the Poor," but this can be approximated.

A more difficult problem will be to estimate the relation between proposed policy changes and changes in the allocation of the national output. Economists have devoted much effort to estimating the consequences of various tax changes on savings, consumption, investment, and economic growth. Although these estimates are much in dispute, there is at least the beginning of an analytical base on which the president and Congress can rely. Less work has been done on what might be called the "incidence" of the expenditure side of the budget. We will have to learn more about this if we are to have a better idea of what the vast federal government is doing.

The connection between government actions and the allocation of the national output is highly relevant to intelligent decisions, and we will not be well served by confining our attention to more precise and accurate estimates of less meaningful and potentially misleading magnitudes. In fact, some estimates of the relation between what the government is doing and the allocation of the national output are implicit; they should be made explicit, debated, and used to improve the decisionmaking process. If the president decides that he wants to make this connection explicit, estimates will be made. The estimates will be the subject of argument and of competing research. The estimates will be improved and the decisionmaking process improved with it.

The process suggested here is an application and extension of the process (for deciding on the defense budget) suggested by the Packard commission in 1986:

> Defense planning would start with a comprehensive statement of national security objectives and priorities, based on recommendations of the National Security Council (NSC).
>
> Based on these objectives, the President would issue, at the outset of his Administration and thereafter as required, provisional five-year budget levels to the Department of Defense (DoD). These budget levels would reflect competing demands on the federal budget and projected gross national product and revenues and would come from recommendations of the NSC and the Office of Management and Budget.
>
> The Secretary of Defense would instruct the Chairman of the Joint Chiefs of Staff (JCS) to prepare a military strategy for the national objectives, and options on operational concepts and key defense issues for the budget levels provided by the President.
>
> The Chairman would prepare broad military options with advice from the JCS and the Commanders-in-Chief of the Unified and Specified Commands (CINCs). Addressing operational concepts and

key defense issues (e.g., modernization, force structure, readiness, sustainability, and strategic versus general purpose forces), the Chairman would frame explicit trade-offs among the Armed Forces and submit his recommendations to the Secretary of Defense. The Secretary of Defense would make such modifications as he thinks appropriate and present these to the President.

The Chairman, with the assistance of the JCS and the Director of Central Intelligence, would prepare a net assessment of the effectiveness of United States and Allied Forces as compared to those of possible adversaries. The net assessment would be used to evaluate the risks of options and would accompany the recommendations of the Secretary of Defense to the President.

The President would select a particular military program and the associated budget level. This program and budget level would be binding on all elements of the Administration. DoD would then develop a five-year defense plan and a two-year defense budget conforming to the President's determination.

The President would submit to the Congress the two-year budget and the five-year plan on which it is based. Congress would be asked to approve the two-year budget based upon this plan. It would authorize and appropriate funding for major weapon systems at the two key milestones of full-scale engineering development and high rate production.

DoD would present the budget to Congress on the basis of national strategy and operational concepts rather than line items. The details of such presentation would be worked out by the Secretary of Defense and appropriate committees of Congress.

This process for making defense decisions really requires a parallel process for making other budget decisions. This is even implied in the statement that "these [defense] budget levels would reflect competing demands on the federal budget and projected gross national product and revenues." The president, therefore, should be weighing the defense claims against other claims not only on the budget but also on the GNP—for which he needs a similar assessment for the other claims. In the procedure suggested here, the claim for national security would be weighed not against taxes or Aid to Families with Dependent Children or the deficit but against consumption of poor or middle-income Americans of this generation, or the income of future generations.

The president needs a net assessment process for the other objectives in which he is primarily interested. He needs to identify those objectives and to organize the machinery for informing him about ways of advancing those objectives, and about his options for achieving them through greater or smaller uses of the national output. (Something like this was contemplated when the Domestic Policy Council was established as a counterpart to the National Security Council, but it has never functioned in a systematic, analytical way.)

The president's objectives and plan for the allocation of the national output, at the level of generality suggested here, will presumably remain stable for a considerable period, barring external events like war. One program every four years, in January following an inauguration, should be sufficient. The program might consist of the following:

a. Statement of objectives as described above

b. Plan for affecting the allocation of the national output for the next four years

c. Proposed four-year budget framework

d. Proposed appropriations for the next two years, with any tax or authorization legislation implied by the four-year budget framework

The Plan in Congress

The four-year budget framework would combine aspects of the Gramm-Rudman-Hollings Act, the annual Congressional Budget Resolution called for under present law, and the "summit" agreement on the budget agreed to by Congress and the president in December 1987. Like G-R-H, it would be an act passed by Congress and signed by the president. It would set a multiyear path for the budget deficit but would not arbitrarily require that the deficit reach zero at the end of the plan. Instead, the deficit would be a variable to be determined like other variables. The sequestration process of G-R-H would be eliminated, and it would avoid the error of G-R-H in deciding upon a budget deficit target without having considered the way in which that target would be achieved.

The four-year budget framework would be specified in a level of detail similar to the present Congressional Budget Resolution; that is, it would set outlay amounts for each of the twenty functional categories on the expenditure side of the budget and would prescribe the amount of revenue to be raised. But unlike the Congressional Budget Resolution it would be an act signed by the president and would endure for four years, unless revised.

The four-year framework would have two specific operational consequences. First, a point of order could be raised in the House or the Senate against any proposed legislation that would transgress it. Second, the president would be required to submit appropriation requests and other proposed legislation in accordance with it. He could submit other requests, in addition to these, but he would at least submit one set of appropriate requests conforming to the framework.

Two features of the December 1987 budget summit are incorporated in this proposal. One is a multiple-year decision on major categories; the other is negotiation between congressional leaders and representatives of the president before the budget is submitted. The budget for fiscal 1989, submitted by the president in February 1988, conformed to the December 1987 agreement. In the proposal made here, the new president would have a year in which to develop his own policy and see how far he could come into agreement with the congressional leadership before he submitted his four-year framework and two-year appropriations request.

At present, the administration's appropriations request to Congress contains about a thousand separate accounts. Congress specifies further detail within these accounts, resulting in about five thousand separate expenditure decisions. Some of them are very large, like the $16 billion payroll for the army. Some are for only a few million dollars. (See Table 4.1.)

One of the first steps in budget reform should be an agreement between the president and the Congress to reduce drastically the number of appropriations accounts. This need not reduce the

Table 4.1
Distribution by Size of Congressional Appropriations–1988

	All Accounts	Discretionary Accounts
Less than $1 million	228	137
$1 million to $9.9 million	156	125
$10 million to $99.9 million	254	218
$100 million to $0.9 billion	209	170
$1 billion to $9.9 billion	96	76
Greater than $10 billion	29	10
	972	736

amount of information provided by the administration to Congress. And with appropriations made for two years, Congress will have more opportunity to review actual performance, a function now too often neglected, and in the review it can look beneath the account totals. The current practice of having two committees of 435 and 100 people to manage, in detail, a budget in excess of $1 trillion is counterproductive and should end.

Politically Impossible?

Many of the proposals suggested here may be dismissed as "politically unrealistic." Things are done as they are because some people like to do them that way and will resist or evade doing them any other way. Resistance may be expected mainly from the Congress, but it will also come from the president. The intent of the reform is, insofar as possible, to get the president to recognize that if he gives high priority to some things in the budget he is giving low priority to some others.

The procedure would try to force him to recognize that if he proposes a general tax reduction he is proposing to increase the consumption of most Americans and to reduce something else— public services or private investment, for example. The point of reform is to face the fact that there is no free lunch.

Presidents are generally not very well informed about the consequences of their budget decisions except as they affect other items within the budget. They can see that if one expenditure is increased another must be cut, or the deficit increased or taxes raised. But the real significance of these consequences is seen mainly in terms of what the public will think. The most obvious case is the deficit, the significance of which for the president is mainly that the public thinks deficits are bad, for reasons about which the public is as ill informed as the president. In a somewhat lesser degree this is true of taxation and many kinds of expenditures.

There is nothing in present procedures that requires the president to know the consequences of his budget decisions. Moreover, if he did know them he would have a positive aversion to making them public. The president does not want to be seen as taking anything away from anyone. In the budgets as published there are only winners, no losers, except possibly "Welfare Queens." The requirement to budget the GNP, therefore, showing where the resources will come from to pay for proposed increases, will be difficult for the president.

The proposed reform thus calls for changes in the president's operations that he may not welcome and may try to avoid. But the main obstacle will be Congress. Congress is asked to commit itself to a general framework for four years and to give up micromanagement by accepting biennial budgeting and fewer, larger appropriation accounts.

It would be easy to say that the whole idea is impractical. On the other hand, there is some evidence to suggest that the system is not entirely immovable. The Budget Reform Act of 1974 was a considerable cession of power by committees of Congress. G-R-H was a major commitment by Congress to a five-year program and an agreement by Congress in some circumstances to accept arbitrarily imposed cuts in the expenditure programs they had enacted.

The recent establishment of the National Economic Commission is evidence of congressional dissatisfaction with the present system; in fact Congress seems to recognize that it is to some extent the victim of the system. Even though it gives individual congressmen power they are reluctant to cede, it also exposes them to pressure from particular interest groups that they would prefer to avoid. (That is one benefit of Gramm-Rudman-Hollings, which turned over to an arbitrary process decisions congressmen did not trust themselves to make.) While the present system gives Congress the power to make innumerable little decisions, it does not give them the ability to make the big decisions as well. The present system absorbs too much of their time in minutiae and does not provide them with enough relevant information to make big decisions well.

There has been a great deal of disappointment with recent efforts at budget reform, especially with the 1974 act. Many supporters of the act looked upon it as a way to achieve two objectives—to hold down government spending and to reduce the budget deficit—but it turned out to be "only" a way of implementing a budget policy. It was not a budget policy. And holding down government expenditures and reducing the budget deficit were not the priorities of the president or the Congress. President Reagan's policy was to increase defense expenditures, cut and then hold down taxes, sustain the Social Security program, and, thereafter, to hold down other expenditures and, to the extent that permitted, hold down the deficit. Insofar as Congress had a different policy, it was to sustain the "other" expenditures and cut defense. Only when the deficit reached $200 billion and threatened to explode and when the stock market crashed did reducing the deficit rise toward the top of the list of the government's priorities. The budget-making procedure implemented this policy.

The trouble with the outcomes has not been the procedure. It has been the policy. The object of the suggestions made here is to arrive at better policy by leading the president and the Congress to understand and explain the consequences of their policies more clearly and realistically.

Many complaints about present procedures relate to mechanics—schedules that are not met, appropriations that are not enacted until after the fiscal year has begun, appropriations requests that are late and that must be approved to keep the government from closing down.

While the process looks messy and is to some degree a source of inefficiency, it is not the cause of deficits being too high (or too low), or expenditures or taxes being increased or decreased. These complaints miss an essential point: budget-making is an adversary process, like war. The president and Congress are adversaries, and individual members of Congress are adversaries to each other. The intensity of this adversarial relation fluctuates. The relation may have been particularly warlike during the Reagan administration, but some tension is always present. Congress makes life difficult for the president not simply out of slovenliness but because that is a way of forcing the president's hand. Similarly, the president sets up confrontations with Congress by trying to limit its options. Efficiency is not to be expected from such a relationship. As Professor Frank Knight said, if you want an efficient football game you should put all twenty-two players on the same side of the line. Many suggestions for improving the budget system seem to assume that all the participants can be put on the same side of the line and can be made to cooperate.

That unlikely assumption is not part of this proposal. Rather, it is assumed that the participants will try to cheat, to evade their commitments, to disguise their intentions, and to limit the options of their adversaries. The object is to change the terms of the struggle and to enable more participants to engage in it. It is to raise the decisionmaking level to a point where more people can see their interests and be informed. It is to change the argument over whether or not to run a deficit into an argument about whether or not to reduce private productive investment and the incomes of our grandchildren. The latter form of the argument increases the number of people who can have an informed opinion rather than respond more or less strongly to some shibboleth. Similarly, the object is to change the argument about taxes from an ideological question to the pragmatic one of the desirability of reducing the growth rate of private consumption or of having some other real effect. At another level, the object is to subordinate the argument about whether or not to spend $3 million on cranberry research to a larger argument about how much of the national output should be devoted to research.

If the kinds of changes described here are desirable, the question is how to get them started. The description begins with the president laying out his idea of the national objectives, of the allocation of the national output required to advance those objectives, and then of the budget that furthers those objectives. But the president is not likely to want to do that. It is too revealing of the costs of his proposals in real terms, and of the objectives that must be sacrificed if his priorities are to be achieved.

Despite the limitations these reforms would place on his freedom to maneuver, a president might find it useful, even liberating, to adopt the line of thinking proposed here. He may find that the deficit and popular notions about it, as well as commitments on taxation, are so confining that no amount of evasion or concealment will allow him to do things he urgently wants to do with respect to defense, infrastructure, education, or other programs. Then he may want to use the budgeting process suggested here to confront the country with its real choices. But that is not the most likely possibility. It is even less likely that the initiative would come from the congressional leadership.

The most hopeful route to improving the budget process is through example and pressure from the private sector. There are many respected and listened-to institutions and individuals outside the government that are intensely interested in the general outlines of budget policy. If they began to discuss the budget as an instrument for advancing basic national objectives by affecting the way in which the national output is allocated among alternative uses, that could become the way that politicians will have to think and talk about the problem.

Initiative for budget reform has come from the private sector in the past. In fact, there was a decade of private discussion and agitation before the executive budget was instituted in 1921. In the postwar consensus period, private advocacy led to the use of the cash-consolidated budget (now called the unified budget), the use of the full-employment budget, and the presentation of five-year budgets. The National Economic Commission is a promising forum in which new ideas for managing the budget can have a hearing, and possibly an endorsement from people whose opinion matters but who do not all have the inhibitions of politicians in office or seeking office.

Of course, there will be no initiative from the private sector—at least of the kind suggested here—unless there is agreement that the budget issue is primarily an issue involving allocation of the national output. There must be people who want to get beyond talking about deficits, taxes, and government expenditures and who believe that the present system neglects to provide for the future, to provide for the national security, to provide for the very poor, or to provide incentives to work and save. That is, they may differ about what is wrong, but will agree that it is time to change the terms of the debate and raise it to a higher level.

• 5 •
Budgets for the 1990s

At this point I want to illustrate as specifically as I can the application of the way of thinking about the budget that has been described in the preceding pages.*

The basic point of the preceding pages is that budgetary decisions should be made according to (a) a view of the national objectives and (b) a view of the relation between budgetary policies and the achievement of those objectives.

People will disagree about the ordering of objectives. There is no budget that is best for everyone. Some people would argue that homelessness is a greater threat to America than the Soviet Union and would want the budget to reflect that. People with the opposite priorities would want a different budget. It is the function of government to resolve differences of whose priorities get most attention in the budget according to the procedures laid down in the Constitution.

But the choice of a budget does not depend only on the choice of objectives. It depends also on an estimate of the relation between budgetary policies and those objectives. To say that a major national objective is to improve the lot of poor people leads to the question whether that objective will be better advanced by

---

* I say "as specifically as I can" in recognition of the limited amount that one researcher and one assistant can know about the vast, complicated federal budget. If the procedures suggested here were to be implemented, much more talent would of course be devoted to it, in and out of the government. The crudity of the calculations presented here should not be taken as evidence of the feasibility of the proposal.

increasing public expenditures for the poor or by reducing them. Similarly, if the rate of growth of the national income is to be increased, is that objective achieved by raising taxes or by reducing them? These are critical questions for which we do not have very good answers. They differ, however, from questions about priorities, which are intrinsically unanswerable. Answers to questions relating means to ends are just not very reliable. The suggestion of this book is to raise the questions—and put them at the forefront of budget decisionmaking—in order to improve the reliability of answers. Meanwhile, however, we have to do the best we can by revealing our estimates and assumptions, to ourselves as well as to each other.

I will try to illustrate the suggested process by presenting four possible sets of priorities for the 1990s and indicating what their implications are for budget policy. The sets of priorities may be briefly described as follows:

a. the priorities implicit in the existing budget programs as reflected in the baseline estimates of the Congressional Budget Office published in February 1988

b. priorities that would place a higher emphasis on defense and investment and much less on the consumption of Americans who are not poor

c. priorities making investment the primary goal and accepting the existing defense program

d. priorities that highlight social concerns—the condition of the poor, education, and health—and substantially deemphasize defense

To put these alternatives in context, it is helpful to see how the national output has been allocated in recent years. Choices for the future depend on how we would like to change the recent trends.

Table 5.1 shows the estimated percentage allocation of the national output among the categories of use that seem most rele-

Table 5.1
Uses of the GNP: 1973, 1980, and 1986 (percent distribution)

	1973	1980	1986
Defense	5.7	5.2	6.6
Education	6.4	6.2	6.2
Other consumption	62.5	64.3	66.9
Health	7.5	8.7	10.3
By poor	1.6	2.0	1.9
By nonpoor	53.4	53.6	54.7
Investment owned			
by Americans	20.1	18.5	14.3
Federal capital	0.3	0.3	0.3
State and local capital	1.9	1.9	1.8
Private domestic capital	17.3	15.8	15.7
Net foreign capital	0.7	0.5	– 3.4
[Investment in America]	[19.5]	[18.0]	[17.7]
Other government	4.7	5.1	5.2
Federal	1.3	1.5	1.3
State and local	3.4	3.6	3.8
Government transfers and			
interest abroad	0.6	0.7	0.9
Total	100.0	100.0	100.0

Source: All data except consumption by the poor from Bureau of Economic Analysis, Department of Commerce, The National Income and Product Accounts of the United States, 1929-82 (Washington, D.C.: U.S. Government Printing Office, 1986), and Survey of Current Business, July 1987. Consumption by the poor estimated by the author using U.S. Bureau of the Census, Money Income and Poverty Status of Families and Persons in the U.S.: 1986 (Washington, D.C.: U.S. Government Printing Office, 1987); Characteristics of Households and Persons Receiving Selected Noncash Benefits: 1984 (Washington, D.C.: U.S. Government Printing Office, 1986); and The Budget of the United States Government for fiscal years 1973, 1980, and 1986 (Washington, D.C.: U.S. Government Printing Office, 1972, 1979, and 1985).

Note: Data may not add to 100 because of rounding.

vant to decisions. I recognize that the selection of these categories is itself a judgment about what the major national issues are—those with different views would look at different categories.

What the table calls "investment owned by Americans" equals private domestic investment plus government investment in fixed capital—roads, dams, etc.—other than defense equipment, minus the net inflow of capital from abroad. I use this number, rather than the more usual figure of investment *in* America, because it is the investment *owned by Americans* that will yield investment income to Americans in the future. Investment in America contributes to the labor income of Americans even if the investment is owned by foreigners because it contributes to the productivity of American workers. That amount is shown in brackets.

The reduction in the share of the GNP going to "investment owned by Americans"—from 20.1 percent in 1973 to 18.5 percent in 1980 to 14.3 percent in 1986—was the outstanding change in the use of the national output during this period. The effect of this on investment in America was cushioned by a big increase in the capital inflow, but even investment in America declined as a share of GNP. *Net* investment owned by Americans—that is, investment after allowance for capital consumption by depreciation and obsolescence—almost disappeared as a fraction of GNP, falling from 11 percent in 1973 to 2.5 percent in 1986.

The decline in investment resulted in part from a decline in the ratio of private saving to GNP, from 18 percent in 1973 to 16 percent in 1986. But much of it was due to the rise in the federal deficit from 0.4 percent of GNP in 1973 to 4.8 percent in 1986. This deficit had to be financed out of private saving, which was then not available for investment.

The decline in the share of GNP going to investment owned by Americans was approximately matched by the increase in the share going to consumption. This was partly the result of the decline in the private saving rate, but mostly the result of the operation of the federal budget. *Net* federal taxes—federal taxes minus federal transfer payments—declined from 12.5 percent of GNP in 1973 to 10.4 percent in 1986. The composition of this decline changed during the period. Between 1973 and 1980 taxes rose as a percentage of GNP, from 19.4 percent to 20.3 percent, but transfers rose even faster, from 6.9 percent to 9.0 percent. Between 1980 and 1986 taxes declined, from 20.3 percent to 19.5 percent, while transfers hardly increased—from 9.0 percent to 9.1 percent.

Almost two-thirds of the increased share of consumption in the GNP took the form of an increased share of expenditures for health care. This was also strongly induced by federal programs, not only Medicare and Medicaid but also provision for the deductibility of medical expenses and the exclusion of medical fringe benefits from taxation.

As shares of GNP, expenditures for defense, education, and consumption by the poor (other than for health) have stayed within a narrow range.

The question that should determine budget policy now, at least in its broadest outlines, is how this allocation of the national output among these major uses should change in the years ahead, if it should change at all.

From the "present" budget policy described in the "baseline" projection of the Congressional Budget Office, and on reasonable assumptions, one can speculate on the allocation of the national output that would emerge five years from now. That projection essentially carries forward the expenditures and revenues that would result from existing legislation or, where existing legislation does not control, assumes constant expenditures in real terms. Thus, the increase of Social Security expenditures is accounted for, as is the increased interest due to the increasing debt and the increased revenue due to the estimated increase in the national income. Defense expenditures are assumed to be constant in real terms.

An estimate of the allocation of the national output in 1993 that would emerge from the baseline budget projection is shown in the first column of Table 5.2.

Because of the projected decline in the budget deficit as a percentage of GNP, the ratio of investment owned by Americans to GNP would rise but would still be significantly below the levels of 1980 and 1973. The rise in the investment share would be approximately matched by a decline in the defense share and a small decline in federal services not elsewhere accounted for (i.e., government expenditures other than for defense, health, education, transfer payments, interest, and fixed capital). The share

Table 5.2
GNP in 1993 (percent distribution)

	Case A Baseline	Case B	Case C	Case D
Defense	5.5	6.4	5.5	4.5
Education	6.4	6.5	6.4	6.7
Other consumption	66.0	62.7	62.8	65.5
Health	12.5	11.2	11.2	12.7
By poor	2.0	2.1	2.0	2.3
By nonpoor	51.5	49.5	49.6	50.6
Investment owned				
by Americans	16.8	19.0	20.2	18.0
Federal capital	0.3	0.3	0.3	0.3
State and local capital	1.9	1.9	1.9	1.9
Private domestic				
capital	15.0	17.2	18.2	16.1
Net foreign capital	− 0.4	− 0.4	− 0.4	− 0.4
[Investment in				
America]	[17.2]	[19.6]	[20.4]	[18.4]
Other government	4.5	4.5	4.5	4.5
Federal	1.0		1.0	1.0
State and local	3.5	3.5	3.5	3.5
Government transfers				
and interest abroad	0.8	0.8	0.8	0.8
Total	100.0	100.0	100.0	100.0

of consumption would be essentially unchanged, but the part going to health would continue to rise.

The estimate of investment assumes that gross private saving will remain at 15.5 percent of GNP, the average of the actual 1986 and 1987 figures. Since there is general agreement that the inflow of capital will decline, the assumption here is that it will decline steadily from $157 billion in 1987 to $25 billion (in 1993 dollars) by 1993. This arbitrary assumption is made only to register the belief that there is no necessary reason for the capital inflow to fall to zero, despite the common assumption to that effect. The assumption does not affect the investment owned by Americans, but it does affect the investment in America. On this assumption, investment in America as a fraction of GNP would still be less than in 1986 and even farther below the 1980 and 1973 figures.

Case A. If the CBO budget represents a satisfactory allocation of the national output, then the budget policy assumed in the projection is also satisfactory in its general outlines. There are, however, many possible standpoints from which this allocation, and the budget policy associated with it, may be considered unsatisfactory. I shall present three cases as illustrations of what I believe to be the main issues, and thus the main priorities, for the country. Case B is my own set of priorities; Cases C and D represent other widely held positions.

Case B. The big danger inherent in the CBO baseline budget, and in recent thinking about the nation's needs, is that inadequate provision will be made for the national security. The freezing of real defense expenditures (in the CBO projections) is not based on any evaluation of our national security requirements but rather on the assumption that Congress will not continue to fund increases for these expenditures. And the unwillingness of Congress to provide more defense funds is also not the result of any appraisal of our defense needs but rather the result of a judgment that we cannot afford more. But since the United States is currently spending only a little more than 6 percent of GNP for defense, that is not a serious proposition. What the judgment really reflects is the sense of Congress that we do not prefer to spend more for defense but would rather have a faster growth of private consumption or of investment or of something else. It implies a low ranking of defense expenditures in the scale of national priorities, but these priorities are rarely explicitly stated and argued.

The (negative) case for more defense is thus partly a case against more of other things—to which I shall turn below. The (positive) case for more defense is supported by studies that reveal the continued inferiority of U.S. forces relative to those of the Soviets, despite the defense buildup of recent years. The need for continued increase in real defense spending was demonstrated in a recent study by the Commission on Integrated Long-Term Strategy, a bipartisan group of highly respected national security experts. They said:

> If we hold [defense spending] at around a 6 percent share of GNP, the United States will be able to increase real defense spending at the long-term growth rate of the economy—3 percent or so a year. At that rate, we could acquire the systems needed to maintain the current worldwide posture, cope with some occasional new threats, and retain some needed flexibility. We could also incorporate the capabilities called for in this report. But if defense cutbacks continue, and we drift to lower levels of GNP share, something will have to give.[1]

The main reason for dissatisfaction with the priorities implicit in the CBO budget baseline is inadequate provision for national defense. There are, however, other reasons as well. The increase in investment, both investment owned by Americans and investment in America, is still very little, coming after a period of slow productivity growth and slow increase in the capital stock. The importance of trying to revive the growth of productivity is accentuated by the fact that we have to look forward to a period in which the number of retired people will be rising rapidly relative to the number of working people.

The educational attainment of the American population is unsatisfactory and is a cause for national concern. This concern is often put in terms of effects on productivity and competitiveness.

The concern with productivity is legitimate; the concern with competitiveness, in my opinion, is not. But beyond economic considerations there is ground for real concern about the effect of an uneducated, even illiterate, population on the quality of life in America. As Thomas Jefferson said, "Whoever expects to be ignorant and free in a state of civilization expects what never was and never will be."

There is some disagreement about whether the improvement of education requires an increase in national expenditures for education. The argument here is much like the argument about defense: undoubtedly, the defense program could be run more efficiently than it is, and the present level of security could be achieved with smaller expenditures. But we cannot defend the country with theoretical efficiencies or educate people with reforms that have not been implemented. If we start with the present educational system and want to make a significant improvement, we will probably have to increase educational expenditures, while simultaneously striving for reforms in methods and content.

Increased expenditures for education may not imply increased *federal* expenditures for education. Despite some expansion, the federal government still supplies only a tiny fraction of total education expenditures. Perhaps the federal government could exercise leadership to encourage more expenditure on education by states, localities, and private citizens without increasing its own expenditures. But an increase in national expenditure for education may have budgetary implications for the federal government even if there is no increase in federal spending. According to the proposal in this book, the appropriate size of the federal deficit or surplus depends on the size of saving by the private sector and by state and local governments (because the deficit or surplus is an influence on the rate of total investment, and the smaller the amount of private and state and local saving, the greater the need for a federal surplus). Therefore, if education expenditures are increased by a reduction of state surpluses or private saving, the appropriate size of the federal deficit will be reduced.

A fourth major national priority—in addition to defense, investment, and education—should be to improve the condition of people living in poverty in the United States, by reducing their number and raising their incomes. Between 1973 and 1986 the number of people in poverty increased from twenty-three million to thirty-four million, or from 10.8 percent of the population to 13.9 percent, even though the poverty line for deciding who was poor was fixed in real terms while average per capita incomes were rising.

Again, it is important to recognize that when some objectives are given higher priority, others get a lower priority. That is what budgeting is all about. In my view, two major uses of the national output deserve lower priority than those just listed. One is expenditure for medical care. Health expenditures as a percentage of GNP and real health expenditures per capita are much higher in the United States than in other industrial countries, without any evidence of a higher standard of health here. Our public and private systems of health insurance seem to encourage wasteful expenditures for medical care. Yet under present arrangements, the share of the GNP devoted to health will continue to rise.

The largest use of the national output by far is the consumption of the 87 percent of the population who are not poor. Between 1973 and 1986 real per capita consumption by the part of the population that is not poor, other than their consumption of health services, increased by 1.7 percent per year, while real per capita output increased by 1.3 percent per year. It is here— and in expenditures for health—that we could best restrain the use of the national output in order to increase the resources devoted to defense, investment, education, and the incomes of the poor.

Column B of Table 5.2 shows a distribution of the GNP that is consistent with this set of priorities. Its basic characteristics are that real defense expenditures have been raised by 3 percent per annum from 1988, that the ratio of health expenditures to the GNP has been frozen at its 1988 level, and that real per capita consumption by the nonpoor (other than health) has also been frozen at its 1988 level. (Nominal increases in education and in consumption by the poor are shown just to indicate that they are subjects worth positive attention but not big claimants on the national income.) Everything else, except private domestic capital investment, is as in the baseline. Essentially this program transfers 3.3 percent of GNP (in the baseline budget) from health and consumption by the nonpoor to defense and investment.

(It should be noted that the real GNP is considered to be the same in all of the hypothetical cases described. This seems a good enough assumption for the short period considered here. Investment will be higher in the three alternative cases, which might be expected to increase real output some by 1993. But taxes will also be higher in the three alternative cases, which may reduce saving and work effort. Which effect would dominate in a five-year period is hard to say. I should expect the growth-increasing effect of continuous higher investment to dominate in the longer run.)

Case C. Undoubtedly the most controversial aspect of the preceding program is its emphasis on increasing defense expenditures. Case C presents a more conventional view of the matter. It relies on the belief that the buildup of the U.S. defense establishment achieved so far and promised by a steady level of spending has accomplished its main objectives, as evidenced by the willingness of the Soviets to negotiate arms reduction and to behave more peacefully in other respects. In this view, the country's main need is to revive economic growth, and its highest priority to increase the rate of investment.

Column C of the table expresses this point of view. It would raise investment owned by Americans to 20 percent of GNP, which was the 1973 rate. This would be accomplished by restraining health expenditures and other consumption by the nonpoor. Otherwise, it is the same as the baseline pattern.

Case D. This places much more emphasis on redistribution than the other programs. It is modeled in a general way on recent proposals of the Reverend Jesse Jackson. Reflecting much skepticism about the need for defense expenditures, this would freeze defense spending in nominal terms, implying a decline of real expenditures by about 17 percent below the baseline by 1993. Cuts would also be made in consumption by the rich. The resources saved from defense and consumption by the rich would be devoted to education and training, health, assistance to the poor, and increasing investment, although the increase of investment would be less than in Cases B and C.

These views of the nation's priorities for the allocation of the national output have general implications for the federal budget. The most obvious is the required size of the budget surplus or deficit. This will depend on the level of private and state and local saving. That is, the required federal surplus will equal (a) the target for investment owned by Americans, minus (b) government capital formation and private and state and local saving. On my assumptions (b) equals 18.7 percent of GNP. Therefore, the baseline case implies a deficit of 1.9 percent of GNP and Case D a deficit of 0.7 percent of GNP, while Case B requires a surplus of 0.3 percent of GNP and Case C a surplus of 1.3 percent of GNP. Translated into 1993 dollars these amounts are:

Case A, baseline $123 billion deficit
Case B $20 billion surplus
Case C $86 billion surplus
Case D $46 billion deficit

At this stage in history, the idea that we should have a surplus may seem fantastic. It is worth noting, however, that this surplus, even in Case C, would just equal the surplus in the off-budget accounts, mainly Social Security, so that the on-budget accounts would be barely in balance. (When the Committee for Economic Development wrote its postwar statement of budget policy in 1947, it recommended a "moderate" budget surplus of $3 billion. That was then about 1 percent of GNP, which would be about $65 billion when applied to the estimated 1993 GNP.)

The budget problems of Case B and Case C are very similar. Although Case C requires a larger budget surplus, Case B requires larger expenditures for defense and, in a token amount, for assistance to the poor. (The small increase in the share going to education is assumed to be financed by state and local taxes.) In each case, about 3.2 percent of GNP, or about $210 billion in

1993, needs to be shifted to the combination of defense and investment. Again, this may seem impossible. But that is only another way of saying that the priorities implied in the hypothetical programs are not acceptable. If increasing defense and investment combined by 3.2 percent of GNP is more important than having that much expenditure on health and other consumption, then the budget problem can be solved by tax and expenditure changes that would restrict the low-priority uses. If these priorities are not accepted, then the budget requirements are different.

The budget problem of Case D seems easier because it does not require as much restraint on private consumption as Case B or C. But D is really easier only if the sacrifice of defense and investment does not have seriously adverse consequences.

If the priorities are accepted, the question will remain, which budget changes should be made to affect them? There are many possibilities. There are possibilities if the desirability of restricting health expenditures and consumption by the nonpoor is accepted. In that case a wide variety of expenditure reductions and tax increases are possible, and choices should be guided by considerations of efficiency and equity. Disincentives to work, save, and produce should be avoided, as should steps that would violate the country's standards of fairness. On all these matters there are, of course, differences of opinion.

I do not intend to make recommendations, but simply to indicate the existence of options that add up to a large amount of money, and that can reasonably be considered consistent with requirements of efficiency and equity. (The list in Table 5.3 is—with one exception, agriculture—derived from a much longer list included in the March 1988 report of the Congressional Budget Office. I should emphasize that the CBO did not endorse any of these options but supplied the estimates of their effects on receipts or expenditures.)

The total of this list, together with the savings of interest that would result from the lower deficits over the years 1989-93 would approximately meet the budget requirements of Case B and well exceed the budget requirements of Case C.[2] Undoubtedly, there

Table 5.3
Possible Expenditure-Reducing or Revenue-Raising Measures
Estimated 1993 effect ($ billion)

Raise premiums to cover 50 percent of cost of Medicare Supplementary Medical Insurance	18.6
Establish new fee schedule for physicians under SMI	10.0
Increase the Medicare deductible	3.6
Tax employer-paid health insurance as income	25.1
Eliminate agricultural income supports	15.0
Tax 60 percent of all Social Security benefits as income	11.3
Eliminate deductibility of state and local taxes	32.1
Limit the value of the mortgage interest deduction to 15 percent of interest	14.5
Tax capital gains at death	5.8
Tax 30 percent of capital gains from home sales	7.5
Increase the motor fuel tax by 12 cents a gallon	11.7
Double the cigarette tax	3.0
Raise tax on distilled spirits by 20 percent and equalize tax on beer and wine with tax on distilled spirits	4.8
Decrease limits on deduction of contributions to pension funds and profit-sharing funds	3.4
Reduce costs of miscellaneous economic subsidies, such as for Export-Import Bank, Rural Electrification Administration, Davis-Bacon Act	3.6
	170.0

Source: Congressional Budget Office, "Reducing the Deficit: Spending and Revenue Options," Washington, D.C., 1988

would be strong opposition to every item on this list, which is why they have not been adopted. But opposition should not be confused with "national interest" arguments about economic efficiency or equity. Opposition would only mean that many people do not accept the priorities of Case B or Case C insofar as they conflict with their own interests.

The purpose of this discussion is not to argue for a specific set of priorities or budget measures but to emphasize that budget discussions should reflect explicit choices about national objectives and priorities in the use of national output.

Part II
The Budget and
Economic Stability

· 6 ·
The Search for a
Stabilizing Budget Policy

$\mathbf{A}$t the end of World War II there was common agreement—at least among people who think of such things—about what the budget problem was and how to deal with it. The nation's chief problem, and objective, was to maintain high employment. This was a natural priority after the miseries of unemployment in the 1930s and the blessings of full employment during the war.

The budget was the main focus for thinking about high employment. The idea that fiscal policy was the government's principal instrument for affecting the rate of employment or unemployment had achieved widespread acceptance after the publication of Keynes's *General Theory* in 1936. The theory seemed to have been confirmed by the war, when a big increase in government spending and government deficits was associated with reduction of unemployment to an extremely low level.

Thus, since high employment was the main national goal and the budget was the main way to achieve it, high employment was the main goal of budget policy. Another subject to which considerable attention was paid was the nature of the tax structure after military spending declined. Business organizations tried to demonstrate the adverse national consequences of high business taxation, but, unlike today, the size and distribution of federal expenditures were not the object of much discussion.

The influence of the budget on the allocation of the national output was not a big issue. The common expectation was that federal spending would decline to 10 percent of GNP, down from the 40-45 percent of the peak war years. The budget would still be much larger, relative to GNP, than before the depression, but that was largely due to higher interest and national security expenditures, residues of the war. No one foresaw that the peacetime budget would grow to 25 percent of GNP and be a dominant factor in the provision of health and educational services and in the flow of income to large sectors of the population.

The main focus, then, was on budget policy as an instrument for maintaining high employment, or, a little more broadly, on stabilizing the economy. The same Keynesian reasoning that indicated the power of fiscal policy also suggested how the power should be harnessed to achieve the objective. In its simplest form, the prescription was that the government deficit should be raised when expansion of the economy was desired and reduced when restraint was the objective.

The simplest prescription was soon recognized to be too simple and inadequate, mainly because of the forecasting problem. Decisions to alter the size of the budget deficit would take time—at least many months—to effectuate after the need was determined, and another substantial delay would be encountered before the budget changes would have their effects on the economy. Consequently, unless the need for stimulating or restraining the economy was accurately seen well in advance, the actions taken would often turn out to be wrong and could make the economy less rather than more stable. The fallibility of economic forecasts had been vividly demonstrated at the end of the war, when economists almost universally forecast a serious recession that did not occur. Indeed, some people believed that forecasting errors would not be randomly distributed, but rather that governments would have a bias toward projecting economic conditions that justified increasing expenditures or cutting taxes.

These concerns led to a common prescription that relied heavily on the automatic variations in revenue and expenditures that come with economic fluctuations. As the economy declined, revenues would also decline, almost simultaneously, while some expenditures, as for unemployment compensation, would rise. These expenditures would tend to moderate the decline by sustaining private incomes. When the economy was rising, there would be a similar movement in the other direction.

The common prescription was that these variations in the budget should be accepted and not offset. There should be no attempt, as there had been in 1932, to counter the recession-induced deficits by raising taxes. The prescription was to live with these automatic variations, but, aside from that, to keep the budget position stable in normal circumstances. A deep and prolonged recession might justify a departure from the standard position. In that case deliberate steps to increase the deficit, beyond the increase that would automatically occur, would be in order. A temporary tax reduction would be the preferred way, although not necessarily the only way, to stimulate the economy.

This formulation required a method for determining when the budget was in the "standard" position that was to be kept stable. The key was to measure the surplus or deficit as it would be if the economy were on some standard and stable path. The surplus or deficit so measured would be kept stable. The *actual* surplus or deficit would depart from the standard as the actual state of the economy departed from its standard.

This strategy was incorporated in recommendations from many sources.[1] A detailed and full articulation of the policy was presented in a 1947 statement by the Research and Policy Committee of the Committee for Economic Development. This version reveals most clearly the nature of the proposed system as well as the difficulties and inadequacies that were encountered and subsequently led to the dissipation of the postwar consensus:

1. Taxes should be set so that they would yield a surplus of $3 billion when the economy is at high employment. (In 1947, $3 billion was over 1 percent of GNP.)

2. High employment is 4 percent unemployment.

3. The budget in which the surplus is to be calculated is the "cash-consolidated" budget. That is, it consolidates the trust accounts—mainly Social Security—with the rest of the budget

and includes all cash receipts and expenditures other than the flows resulting from issuing or retiring Treasury debt.

4. The $3 billion surplus should remain the standard unless there is a "major change in the condition of national life."

5. A temporary departure from the $3 billion surplus standard is permissible when needed to restore economic stability after an extraordinary departure from it, such as a severe recession.

The basic rationale of this fiscal strategy was the Keynesian view that an increase in expenditures and a decrease in revenues (in a recession), whether they occurred automatically or as a result of deliberate action, would sustain total demand for goods and services and thus cushion or reverse the recession. A similar process, in reverse, would operate when the economy was above its target path. Since the strategy placed much emphasis on the variation of tax revenues, the theory assumed a significant and prompt response of private spending to variations in tax payments. An even less activist rationale for the policy as an economic stabilizer was that it sought to avoid disturbances to the economy from the side of the budget, without necessarily claiming that the budget would offer resistance to fluctuations arising in the private sector.

Other benefits were expected from the plan, in addition to its contributions to economic stability, and in the minds of some, but not most, supporters of the plan these other benefits were its chief merits. One of these benefits was to avoid fluctuations in tax rates and expenditures programs that would be disturbing and inefficient. Businessmen particularly were concerned about having to deal with tax rates that would go up and down with fluctuations of the economy. They were as much concerned with the fluctuations in tax rates that would result from an attempt to keep the budget constantly in balance—along traditional lines—as with the fluctuations in tax rates that would result from activist use of taxes to counter every forecast up or down of the economy. Supporters of the plan also recognized how inefficient it would be to try to vary most government spending programs—defense, for example—in response to fluctuations in aggregate economic conditions.

Another expected benefit was that the policy would exert "discipline" over government spending decisions. If the surplus had to be kept constant, an increase of expenditures would have to be balanced by an equal increase of revenues, and government would have to weigh the political unpopularity of raising taxes against the political popularity of increasing spending. Moreover, this discipline would persist through recessions or booms (aside from exceptional circumstances when the standard would be temporarily suspended). Although some expenditures would automatically rise in a recession, an increase in expenditures beyond that would require a tax increase.

This general approach to fiscal policy seemed attractive in the postwar years, as a reconciliation of the new Keynesianism with practical operational concerns and traditional values. Basically, it encouraged the government to accept the deficits that came with recessions but to discourage deficits in what could be considered "normal" times. The idea was first tested in the Eisenhower administration, the first post-Keynesian Republican administration. The question then was how the conservatives would react to a recession. In fact, they did not try to prevent the deficits that occurred in the recessions of 1954, 1957, and 1960. They resisted more positive measures even when there was considerable call to cut taxes in the 1957 recession, the most severe of the postwar period up to that time. And they tried to get back to a balanced-budget position after their recession deficits.

A test from the other direction came with the Kennedy administration. Walter Heller, President Kennedy's chief economic adviser, had earlier commended the CED policy as a considerable step forward but made clear that he did not regard it as having reached the appropriate degree of flexibility and liberation from conventional thinking about balanced budgets. But when the Kennedy administration put forward its proposal for a major tax cut in 1962, it defended the measure on the ground that although the budget was actually in deficit it was in surplus at full employment and would be in balance at full employment after the recommended tax cut. Significantly, the consensus was already undergoing some dilution, because the CED supported the tax cut even though it was inconsistent with its earlier position that there should be a *surplus* at high employment. In 1966 the Johnson administration defended its Vietnam War deficit by saying that the budget would be in balance at full employment, but that was a further dilution of the rule because the budget would then be in balance with full employment *and inflation,* which was not part of the original proposal.

The most formal effort to establish balancing the budget at full employment as the standard of federal fiscal policy came in January 1971, when President Nixon made that one of the key points of his economic and budget program. The president was disappointed to find little commendation for what he regarded as a progressive step. Although the president explained his action by saying, "Now I am a Keynesian," the Keynesians did not welcome him into their club. More traditional people derided the idea of balancing the budget under nonexistent conditions.

The idea of balancing the budget at high employment, but accepting the deficits associated with recession, surfaced again in the Reagan administration during the recession of 1982 and thereafter. The administration pointed out that much of the existing deficit was due to operating below high employment, and made no effort to eliminate that part of the deficit. Rather, it concentrated its recommendations on drastically reducing the deficit that it saw persisting and growing even with high employment in the years ahead. By then the prospective high-employment, or "structural," deficits looked very large, and the administration's proposals did not aim to eliminate them, only to reduce them. Still, the idea was accepted that the standard for appraising the budget position was not the actual deficit or surplus but was the deficit or surplus as it would be under certain hypothetical, but hoped-for, conditions of the economy.

On the whole, one can say that fiscal policy in the postwar period up to the 1980s bore a resemblance to the postwar consensus. We never got very far from balance at high employment, although the idea of a surplus at high employment was lost along the way, and the balance was achieved with the aid of inflation. We never tried to resist the fluctuations of the budget position that came with fluctuations in the economy, and deliberate efforts to stimulate or restrain the economy by fiscal means were small relative to the size of the economy. Failure to adhere to the policy more precisely and systematically can be explained in part by the natural resistance of the political process to any rules. But that failure, and the current neglect of the whole idea of a stabilizing rule of fiscal policy, must be ascribed to certain inadequacies in the original postwar conception and questions about its validity.

1. *Lack of guidance on the size of the surplus or deficit.* The lack of any sound, credible, agreed-upon basis for determining the size of the budget surplus or deficit is one of the main deficiencies in budget policy in the 1980s. The importance of this lack was not so conspicuous forty years ago, but it gradually became clearer and clearer.

The early formulations, calling for a balanced budget or "small" surplus at high employment, rested on several propositions. The key, stabilizing aspect of the policy did not depend on the size of the standard surplus or deficit at high employment, but only required that the size of the standard surplus or deficit be constant, so that variations would be correlated with departures from high employment. From this standpoint, it did not matter whether the budget went from a surplus of $3 billion at 4 percent unemployment to a deficit of $3 billion at 5 percent unemployment or from a deficit of $5 billion at 4 percent unemployment to a deficit of $11 billion at 5 percent unemployment. Also, from the standpoint of discipline over expenditures, the size of the standard deficit or surplus did not matter. As long as the standard was constant the policy required balance at the margin; that is, expenditure increases would have to be matched by revenue increases.

If constancy of the standard was the essential thing the standard would have to command popular support, to resist political temptations to depart from it. The standard of a balanced budget was clearly the standard most likely to command such support, and proponents of the postwar strategy believed that the support was very strong. They thought that to propose a standard deficit would have been unacceptable. Or, if they had managed to make the idea of a standard deficit acceptable, they would not have been able to locate any stopping point, any way to keep the acceptable deficits from getting bigger and bigger. In fact, one of the most appealing features of the postwar strategy was that it moored itself to what was thought to be the public's nearly religious belief in budget balancing while rejecting the Hoover-like folly of trying to balance the budget in recessions. The framers of the strategy did not feel the need to explain why the budget should be balanced. They thought the public was committed to that idea and they wanted to make use of the commitment. What explanation they would have given is unclear.

Public commitment to a balanced budget may have been the reality in the days before the depression and before Keynes, when federal budgets were, in fact, generally balanced. But that may be less evidence of the strength of the commitment to budget balancing than of the weakness of the strain put on that commitment. The growth of the economy was rapidly raising revenues while demands that could be legitimately placed on the federal government were still quite limited. Balancing the budget was fairly easy.

After World War II the balanced budget became a flag more often saluted than followed, as I said in *The Fiscal Revolution in America*. In opinion polls, two-thirds of the respondents always said that the budget should be balanced. But they never elected presidents or congressmen who would balance the budget or unseated those who didn't.

Moreover, if there was an intuitive attachment to the idea of a balanced budget, it was not readily transferred to the idea that the budget should be balanced at some hypothetical state of the economy. That became clear when the financial and business community rejected President Nixon's attempt to establish the rule that the budget should be balanced at high employment. He thought it would be welcomed by the "conservatives" as a way of limiting fiscal manipulation of the economy. Instead they regarded it as an evasion.

A more functional, less traditional approach did not specify how big the budget surplus or deficit should be. The standard prescription of the postwar years was that the surplus or deficit should be big enough to achieve high employment without inflation, or at least the optimum combination of those goals. There were two problems with this prescription. In the first place, no one could calculate reliably what the relation between the budget surplus or deficit and the state of the economy was or would be in the future years for which the budget decisions were being made. But more fundamentally, there was not even a theoretical answer to the question of how high the budget deficit or surplus had to be to achieve high employment without inflation. This became clear as soon as the effect of monetary policy was recognized. The desired aggregate condition of the economy could be achieved with various combinations of monetary and fiscal policy—more money and less deficit or less money and more deficit. Thus, the proper size of the deficit to achieve the desired aggregate economic condition could not be simply estimated (even if we could estimate it) but had to be chosen from a range of possibilities accompanied by complementary monetary policies.

This fact emerged from the "neoclassical" synthesis of Keynesianism and monetarism and was definitively stated by Paul Samuelson in "Principles and Rules in Modern Fiscal Policy: A Neo-Classical Reformation":

> But in any case we are all agreed that over the long run, monetary policy has considerable leverage in helping to determine the mix of high-employment national product between consumption and investment goods of different categories, and that fiscal policy need not take as ultimate data quantitatively predetermined deflationary or inflationary gaps.[2]

This conclusion was not immediately accepted by policymaking economists. In 1970 economists at the Bureau of the Budget resisted the idea that the federal government should run a surplus equal to the surplus in the Social Security trust funds, on the ground that the economy could not reach high employment with such a surplus. As late as the 1980s the Congressional Budget Office was offering opinions as if the aggregate behavior of the economy was uniquely determined by the path of the deficit. This was increasingly seen to be an unsatisfactory approach.

The postwar consensus was a union of Keynesian functional finance with a popular attachment to balancing the budget. But the Keynesian idea proved inadequate to indicate the proper size of the deficit or surplus, and the popular attachment proved too weak to discipline budget policy. So the whole system was left afloat with respect to this crucial element of policy.

This did not deny the validity of the idea that the size of the surplus or deficit should be constant when the economy was in its standard condition—typically defined as high employment— and should depart from that constant when the economy departed from that standard condition. It meant that the location of that constant surplus or deficit had no firm basis either in sentiment or in economics and therefore could not be expected in practice to remain constant.

Thus, one of the anchors of the postwar consensus—an agreed-upon, constant size of the deficit or surplus to be achieved as the standard condition of the economy—was gone. If that had to be argued every year, and possibly varied every year, the automatic stabilizing character of the system would be severely damaged.

2. *Uncertainty about the "standard" path of the economy.* A basic element of the postwar consensus was that the budget position should be constant when the economy was on its desired path so that variations in the budget position would not disturb it but would help restrain departures from it. The desired path was then described as "high employment" or "full employment," conventionally thought to be 4 percent unemployment.

By around 1960 some disagreement arose about whether full employment was 3 percent, 4 percent, or 5 percent unemployment. It did not matter in principle as long as the correct number was a constant, although the fact of disagreement opened up the possibility that political debate over stimulative policy would reappear as a debate about what full employment was. A more serious conceptual question emerged when it appeared that "high employment" was a number that changed, for demographic and other reasons. It greatly complicated the notion and increased the room for dispute about what the standard was.

Further difficulties appeared as efforts were made to apply the idea of the standard surplus, notably in the early days of the Nixon administration. Earlier formulations assumed that the automatic variations in the surplus or deficit would be simple functions of the unemployment rate. But the budget position depended more on the national income, which did not have a constant relation to the unemployment rate. Some notion of trend or potential national income seemed more relevant than "high employment," but that raised other estimating problems. Most important, upon examination, the high-employment path or the trend path of real output turned out not to be the path that policy should always try to keep the economy on. In the early 1970s we began to encounter conditions in which the desired path of the economy would run below high employment or the output trend in order to get the inflation rate down. The belief was that a temporary period of "low" employment and output and low inflation would eliminate inflationary expectations and then permit high employment to be regained on a gradual path without reigniting the inflation. This turned out to be only one example of possible cases in which some transition to the desired condition of budget balance at high employment would be required. The general rule provided no guidance for that transition.

3. *Inability to deal with the inflation problem.* The idea that the budget should be balanced at high employment implied that departures from high employment could be and would be on both sides. There would be deficits when the economy was below high employment and surpluses when the economy was "above" high employment. But above high employment was mainly inflation.

The theory was that surpluses "above" high employment would tend to restrain inflation. But the policy did not tell how big the surplus should be at high employment with different amounts of inflation.

This problem surfaced in the early days of the Vietnam War, when employment was high and inflation was also reaching figures that seemed exceptionally high at the time. The Johnson administration claimed that its budget policy was adequate because the budget was balanced at high employment. Critics said that the policy was inadequate because the balance was achieved only with inflation. An effort then ensued to discover how to measure what the surplus would have been "without inflation." Did it mean at the price level of the previous year, a year before the inflation started, or some other year? Or did it mean at the inflation rate of the previous year? No answer was found that was not arbitrary.

Around 1980 a different aspect of the inflation question surfaced. Some economists maintained that inflation actually made the deficit smaller than the conventional measurement because it reduced the real value of the debt and some of the interest the government paid was only an offset to the real gain on the debt. This argument also remained unsettled, but it further complicated the application of the budget-balancing rule. In addition, if inflation was actually considered to reduce government expenditures by reducing real interest payments, and therefore to reduce the amount of taxation needed to keep the budget in balance at high employment, it would weaken the built-in anti-inflation effect of the rule.

4. *Doubts about the policy as a stabilizer.* The postwar consensus on fiscal variation embodied two stabilizing elements. The primary one was the automatic variation in the budget position that would accompany fluctuations in the economy. The other was that extraordinary, deliberate fiscal action would be taken in extraordinary circumstances—that is, when departures from the desired path of the economy were so big and clear that the danger of destabilizing the economy by taking the wrong action was small.

In fact, the identification of these extraordinary circumstances turned out to be difficult. The first important case was the 1957-58 recession, the worst up to that time since World War II. Some supporters of the consensus rule thought that was the time to invoke the extraordinary action. But even as that was being debated the economy was beginning a sharp upturn, as later information revealed.

Questions were also raised about the automatic stabilizing aspects of the policy. At first these questions only related to the size of the stabilization effect. The proposition, generally accepted by 1960, that consumption depended on permanent incomes suggested that the automatic but temporary change in tax liabilities and transfer payments in a recession would have little effect on consumption. This effect was made to seem even smaller by the theory, which became increasingly influential after about 1975, that a deficit created in a recession, even if created automatically, would not help sustain the economy, because taxpayers would recognize the future tax liability and would regard that as an offset to current tax savings.

These arguments did not, however, invalidate the case for keeping tax rates and expenditure programs stable and accepting the deficits that would automatically result in a recession. The stability of tax rates and expenditure programs could be defended as helpful for efficiency in both the private and public sectors.

More critical questions about the postwar theory of stabilization through fiscal policy emerged in the mid-1980s, when the budget deficit reached about 4 percent of GNP—about $200 billion—at a time generally considered fairly prosperous. Questions arose over whether we could tolerate an increase of the deficit to $300 billion such as might automatically occur in a recession. Would not the sight of such deficits shatter the confidence of investors at home and abroad, causing interest rates to skyrocket and the economy to be further depressed rather than sustained? These concerns raised the possibility that some would advocate a policy of resisting the increase of deficits that would tend to occur in a recession.

A more specific reflection of this appeared after the stock market crash in October 1987, which was considered to threaten the onset of a recession. The almost universal conclusion was that the crash made reduction of the budget deficit imperative. In fact, some suggested cuts of $50 billion a year for three years.

By 1987 many people rejected both the Keynesian notion that deficits stimulated the economy and the monetarist notion that deficits had no aggregate effect. Increasingly, opinion returned to the notion that Herbert Hoover had reluctantly embraced in 1932, that deficits depressed the economy. The postwar consensus on budget policy for economic stabilization had fallen apart.

We have arrived at a condition of great uncertainty about how to adapt budget policy to the fact of unpredictable and undesirable fluctuations of the economy. There is considerable doubt over whether, in principle or in practice, budget policy can contribute to economic stability. And little agreement about how it can contribute, if it can. Nothing has been learned in the past forty years to indicate that the skepticism of fiscal fine tuning that led to the postwar consensus was unjustified. But at the same time, it has become clear that the ideas underlying the postwar consensus were too simple. The notion that there was a national commitment to balancing the budget, which could be translated into a commitment to balancing the budget at high employment, turned out to be wrong. Moreover, whether a commitment to any constant budget position would be a good thing forever became questionable. Even if the idea of holding the budget position constant for some reasonable period of time at a constant condition of the economy was accepted, the definition of that condition appeared to be more of a problem than had first been recognized. It was not only that "high employment" was hard to measure, it also might not be the most relevant concept. And experience has revealed more kinds of situations in which "extraordinary" departures from the basic stabilizing budget rule might be justified than were recognized in the early formulations of the rule.

Recent obsession with the problem of the budget deficit has diverted attention from the question (considered either unimportant or unanswerable) of managing the budget in response to economic fluctuations. But the question will have to be answered somehow.

Nonetheless, the postwar consensus did contain a core of validity; it dealt with a real problem and identified the elements of a solution, which were constancy of the budget position from year to year according to a standard path, suggested but not actually defined by "full employment," with provision for departure from that position under specified conditions. The task now is to reconstruct a policy with those elements in the light of the experience and thinking of the past forty years.

That reconstruction will have to start with a reconsideration of the role of the budget as an economic stabilizer. We have come a long way from the confident belief that we could stabilize the economy by running deficits to prevent recessions and surpluses to moderate booms. Our present state of mind is well represented in the comment of William Beeman, formerly chief economist of the Congressional Budget Office: "We know that there is a deficit multiplier; but we just don't know whether it is positive or negative."

The idea that the multiplier might be negative—that reducing the budget deficit would stimulate the economy and prevent a recession—received more attention after the stock market crash of October 1987 than at any time in the preceding fifty years. The key to the idea was investors' confidence. The crash was seen as evidence that investors' confidence was badly shaken. Unless it was restored, or further deterioration of confidence averted, asset prices would decline, interest rates would rise, and both consumption and investment would be depressed. The loss of confidence that led to the stock market crash was attributed to the deficit, and reduction of the deficit was seen as the essential step for restoring confidence.

The trouble with such arguments is that they are impossible to prove or disprove. The statements of investors about what impairs their confidence are not reliable, nor are the statements by editorial writers and others who claim to speak for investors. There is an overwhelming tendency for everyone to attribute his loss of confidence to the failure of the government to do what he wanted. Thus, the loss of confidence before the stock market collapse was attributed to the suggestion of James Baker, secretary of the treasury, that the dollar might be allowed to decline, to the rejection of Judge Robert Bork's nomination to the Supreme Court, to the prospect of protectionist legislation, to the persistence of the trade deficit, and to a variety of other developments as well as to the budget deficit. No one could disprove the relevance of any of these developments.

The fact is, of course, that anything that impairs confidence will have a negative effect, however unrealistic or irrational the fear may be. But the persistence of unrealistic or irrational fears about budget deficits results from misinformation that should be correctable. Presumably the fear connected with budget deficits is that their continuation will increase the ratio of debt to GNP substantially, causing a large increase of interest rates in the future. The anticipation of future high rates increases present rates, which in turn has other depressing effects. That is, the rational element in the negative effect of deficits is the expectation of future deficits and debts.

Little of that rational element was present in the fall of 1987, before the stock market crash. The ratio of federal debt to GNP had fallen from 100 percent at the end of World War II to 24.4 percent in 1974 and then had risen to 43.2 percent by mid-1987. But by that time the ratio of deficits to GNP was falling, and even on a fairly "pessimistic" estimate, the ratio of debt to GNP would not rise but might well decline. Such a forecast was politically realistic because the operative force was the end of the defense buildup.

But the fear of the deficit in 1987 may have been real, even if not realistic. Under other conditions—in other policy environments—the fear might be realistic. What has the negative effect is not the deficit but the expectation of deficits of such a size and duration as to raise the debt-to-GNP ratio significantly. The key question is whether the fact of current deficits can be separated from the expectation of excessive deficits in the future. The answer seems to be affirmative, in general. For example, the largest Reagan deficit, relative to GNP, coexisted with declining interest rates. If there actually is a negative effect of budget deficits, it seems to be connected with an uncertain political atmosphere. The Carter budget of January 1980 may have been such a case. The deficits then, much smaller than we later became accustomed to, were apparently alarming because they were taken as part of the accumulating evidence of Jimmy Carter's inability to govern. The deficit situation in mid-1987 may have been another case—even though the numbers were not getting worse, the uncertainty about the course of the deficit may have increased. The budget was not running according to the procedures laid down in the Gramm-Rudman-Hollings Act, and the president and Congress seemed incapable of managing anything cooperatively. This uncertainty may have contributed to a rise of interest rates and then to the stock market crash, although this seems a weak hypothesis for so dramatic an event.

Concern about the negative effects of deficits points to the need to provide some assurance that the path of future deficits will be controlled by reasonable and informed evaluation of their effects. A rule requiring the budget to be balanced annually would provide such assurance if it were credible. But such a rule would ignore many other national interests in the budget and precisely for that reason would not be credible. Nor would it be the only rule that would serve the purpose. Rules requiring balance, or a constant deficit, at high employment, or over a period of years, or rules about the ratio of debt to GNP, could also serve.

The main requirement is national understanding of the function and effects of deficits in order to limit their size. One purpose of this book is to help provide that understanding.

On the assumption that such understanding exists, so that deficits, or increases of deficits, do not cause a shock to confidence that depresses the economy, we may now turn to the more conventional version of the relation between budget deficits or surpluses and the level of aggregate demand. The basic proposition of postwar thinking about fiscal policy was that an increase in the deficit would make aggregate demand higher than it would otherwise have been and a decrease in the deficit would have the opposite effect. Using this effect, management of deficits and surpluses could reduce fluctuations in aggregate demand.

The basic proposition and the prescription derived from it have been subject to a number of qualifications.

1. Except in rather unusual circumstances, an increase in the deficit will raise interest rates, curtailing private investment and thus to some extent offsetting the stimulative effects of the deficit increase. More recently, as capital has moved more freely across national borders, this offsetting effect has taken the form of an increase in the exchange rate and a decline in the trade balance. Reducing the budget deficit generates offsetting effects in th other direction. The extent of these offsets is a subject of disagree ment, but the experience and analysis seem to lead to increas ing estimates of the size of the offsets. The size probably depend on a number of conditions, prominent among which would be the accompanying monetary policy. But this suggests the possibility that the desired effects could be achieved by monetary means alone.

2. The hypothesis (the Ricardian or Barro hypothesis) that an increase in the budget deficit will increase private saving may have more realistic implications for short-run stabilization policy than for long-run growth. There has been a tendency, for both administrative and political reasons, to focus on temporary variations of tax rates rather than on expenditures as the preferred means for executing an active fiscal policy to stabilize the economy. But the temporary change in taxes, known to be followed soon by an offsetting change in the other direction, is precisely the kind of change most likely to provoke the Barro response. That is, taxpayers will increase their saving when they get the tax relief because they know that they will soon have to pay higher taxes, and they will reduce their saving when they get the temporary tax increase because they know that tax reduction will soon follow. These offsets are unlikely to be 100 percent, but they will restrain the effect on aggregate demand of temporary changes of tax rates.

3. Experience has demonstrated the difficulty of managing the timing and magnitude of short-run changes in the budget so as to make a contribution to economic stability.

These qualifications do not suggest that it would be wise to try to offset or prevent the built-in variations of revenues and expenditures that accompany cyclical fluctuations in the economy. Even if this automatic variation in the budget had no stabilizing value, the attempt to prevent it would cause unnecessary inefficiency in the operation of government expenditure programs and unnecessary disturbance for taxpayers. And this built-in flexibility of the budget probably does have some stabilizing value, although possibly less than we thought forty years ago.

In recent years, when the "normal" budget deficits under high-employment conditions have been large relative to GNP, concern has been expressed about whether we can "afford" or tolerate the increase in the deficit that would come with a recession. There has also been a tendency to set deficit targets without reference to the expected state of the economy, so that the lower the expected level of national output, the lower the appropriate level of federal spending is thought to be. But nothing in the "normal" level of the budget deficit makes it sensible to try to fight the association of the size of the deficit with the level of the economy. The point that exists in the current concern is properly about the size of the normal deficit, not about the increases that would occur in the recession.

The problem is that the growth of the debt is determined by the actual deficits, not by the deficit that would occur at high employment. If an object of policy is to maintain, or not exceed, some target ratio of debt to GNP, the deficit at high employment must be set so that the actual deficits, taking account of periods of recession, will not push the debt-to-GNP ratio above the target. Thus, suppose that the goal is to keep the debt at 50 percent of GNP. If the economy grows, in nominal terms, by 6 percent a year, the deficit should average 3 percent of GNP. It must average that at the *actual* level of GNP. But if the actual deficit on the average is 50 percent larger than the high-employment deficit, then the high-employment deficit should be 2 percent of GNP. Assume that the object of policy is a budget surplus equal (over a reasonable period of time) to, say, 1 percent of GNP, so that total investment will be equal to private saving plus 1 percent of GNP. Then the high-employment surplus will have to be more than 1 percent of high-employment GNP, to allow for the fact that there will be smaller surpluses, or deficits, when the economy is below high employment.

The present state of knowledge does not rule out the possibility of using deliberate variations of the budget to stabilize the economy. The issue here has always been under what conditions it was likely to be safe and productive. For all the talk we used to hear about "fine tuning," no one ever thought that the budget should be in continuous flux, resisting every movement of the economy. And there were few, if any, who would reject the possible active use of fiscal policy in a situation like 1932. The question is how big a departure from the desired state of the economy, how confidently forecast, is required to justify such a policy. The answer seems to be that the departure has to be quite large and the forecast quite confident. This is especially so because of the doubts now cast on the efficacy of temporary variations of tax rates, which once seemed the most useful instrument for fiscal management. Also, our budgetary situation has become tighter, and the difficulty of reaching soundly based agreement on expenditure and tax programs has become greater, so that injecting the further consideration of short-run stabilization into the decisionmaking process seems less practical and wise. Still, no one can specify how extreme the conditions would have to be. Someone will have to exercise judgment.

· 7 ·
Budgets in an
Unstable Economy

The suggestions made in Part I relate to the long-run or medium-run composition of the budget as it affects the long-run or medium-run allocation of the national output. The president is visualized as submitting a four-year budget to implement his plan. The budget would be broken down into annual (but not necessarily equal) segments, which the president and Congress would be free to alter, but only when there is a serious need to do so.

In an economy that was stable, or even simply predictable, the management of the annual aspects of the longer-run plan would present no special difficulties. But since our economy is neither stable nor predictable, there is a problem of managing the year-to-year movement of the budget with respect to these objectives:

- The efficiency of the government and of the private sector;

- The consistency of the year-to-year movements with the longer-term goals;

- The stability of the economy, which requires at a minimum that the budget should not be a source of instability and, if possible, that the budget should counteract instability arising from the private sector. This goal was, of course, the main concern in the consideration of the economics of fiscal policy in the fifty years after the Great Depression.

A policy to achieve these three objectives should take account of the following facts:

a. Stability of expenditure levels of some government programs is extremely important for efficiency. This has been most clearly demonstrated for the defense program, where short-term instability in the schedules of defense procurement has been found to increase production costs greatly. But it applies to many other programs as well. This cannot, of course, require absolute and permanent constancy of programs once decided upon, but it is a strong argument against changes in response to economic fluctuations that are irrelevant to the purpose of the program.

b. In general, stability of the rates and other terms of taxation is important to the private sector. Taxpayers need to be able to plan on what taxes will be, and they should not be given an artificial incentive to adapt the timing of economic activity to variations in taxes. Stability of some other rates, such as the benefit rates for unemployment compensation, is also important.

c. The combination of desirable stability of the expenditure levels of some programs and desirable stability of tax rates and of some other expenditure programs will result in variations in the budget deficit as the economy fluctuates, variations opposite to the fluctuation of the economy.

d. This combination of stabilities of programs and rates that results in automatic variations in the deficit may contribute to reducing fluctuations in the economy.

e. Further variations in the deficit, beyond those occurring automatically, may on some occasions be helpful in stabilizing the economy but are difficult to manage.

f. Large variations in the overall budget position, or deficit or surplus, that are not adaptations to fluctuations of the economy are probably destabilizing and should be avoided if possible— but it will not always be possible.

g. Short-run, year-to-year variations in the size of the budget surplus or deficit may be important, positively or negatively, for the stability of the economy, but they are not important for the long-term growth of the economy. The average, or cumulative, size of the surplus or deficit is not important for stability but is important for long-run growth because it affects the long-run growth of the stock of productive capital.

We need a budget policy that reconciles our objectives of efficiency, growth, and stability under these conditions, or at least contributes to their reconciliation. The best policy for doing that, as well as the difficulties of doing it, is *suggested* by the postwar consensus rule of setting expenditure programs and tax rates so that the budget would be balanced at high employment. The word "suggested" is emphasized because the strategy cannot literally be that. Important revisions are required:

• "Balanced budget" should be interpreted to mean the chosen target level of the surplus or deficit, which may not be— probably will not be—zero and which is ideally kept constant over several years but not necessarily forever.

• "High employment" should be interpreted as the desirable probable path of the economy, which may not be the high-employment path. It should be the desirable path so that the stabilizing feature of the policy will tend to stabilize the economy around its desired path. It should be the probable path in the sense that deviations from it over a period of years will balance out so that the cumulative budget outcome—the cumulative budget surplus or deficit—over a period of years will probably be the planned outcome.

• The policy must explicitly recognize the role of monetary policy, which was, at most, implicit in the early postwar formulations. It is the responsibility of monetary policy to make the desirable path of the economy the probable path as well. Budget policy alone will not do that. Budget policy will tend to moderate fluctuations of the economy and will avoid disturbances to its path that arise from the budget, but it will not by itself make the desirable path the probable one. (Despite complaints from the Council of Economic Advisers, President Nixon's speechwriters in 1971 insisted on describing the policy of balancing the budget at high employment as a "self-fulfilling prophecy," as if the policy would keep the economy at high employment.)

What was once called a policy of setting expenditure programs and tax rates to balance the budget at high employment needs to be restated as a policy of setting expenditure programs and tax rates to yield a stable surplus or deficit when the economy is on its stable probable path—the size of the surplus or deficit to be decided by the effect of cumulative surpluses or deficits on long-term economic growth. And even this prescription needs to be qualified, namely, that the target surplus or deficit, or "structural" deficit as it has come to be called, cannot literally be a constant for several reasons:

1. The automatic variations of the actual surplus, if the structural one is kept constant, will tend to keep the economy on the desired path if the economy is on the desired path. It will also tend to keep the economy *off* the desired path, if it is off that path, as it will surely be at times. This should not ordinarily be a reason for changing the structural surplus. But there may be times when the economy is far off—presumably below—its target path and is running a large deficit, so that recovery would be seriously impeded if the actual deficit had to be substantially reduced during a rise of the economy. In that case it may be desirable to moderate the rate at which the deficit would have to decline as the economy recovered, and that would mean temporarily increasing the structural deficit.

2. There will be times when the need for changes in expenditure programs or tax rates cannot be accommodated within the confines of the constant structural deficit unless other parts of the budget are seriously disturbed. The most obvious case is war or military buildup, but there may be others. This may be a reason for altering the structural deficit.

3. The structural deficit may initially be at a level that is not desirable on a continuing basis, having reached that point through error or some unforeseen development. In recent years when the structural deficit was in the neighborhood of $200 billion, no one would have said it should be stabilized at that level. A transition to the desired stable level will be necessary.

4. If the economy runs for some time far below its desired path, actual deficits for that period will be far above the desired level. This will imply that the increase in the capital stock during this period has been significantly below what had been expected when the size of the structural surplus or deficit was selected. This may call for a subsequent increase in the structural surplus (or reduction in the structural deficit) to make good that deficiency of investment. If the economy falls significantly below its desired path, despite efforts to keep it there, monetary policy will subsequently have to achieve the desired path with a larger budget surplus or smaller deficit than had been previously planned.

5. The previous situation is one instance of a more general case, which is that ideas of the desirable structural deficit may change because of change in the forecast growth rate or change in the priority assigned to future growth as an objective of national policy. This adds up to a considerable qualification of the rule that the target surplus—the surplus that would be realized if the economy were on its desired path—should be a constant. Nevertheless, there is much value in that rule, and departures from it should be limited. That is, we can say that the target surplus (or deficit) should be constant unless one of a limited number of conditions justifies a change:

a. an extraordinary departure of the economy from its desired path

b. extraordinary changes in expenditure requirements, such as may be associated with a defense emergency

c. an initial surplus position that is far from the desired level in relation to the state of the economy

d. a change in the priority given to long-term growth, and therefore in the target level of the surplus or deficit

Proposals by the president, or anyone else, to change the target surplus should be explicitly defended on one of these grounds. Moreover it will ordinarily be important to move from one level of target surplus to another gradually, to avoid possible disturbance of the path of the economy.

This policy requires us to calculate regularly the size of the deficit or surplus as it would be when the economy was on some desired path, which will not often be where it actually is. Of course, any decisions about the budget, which mean decisions about the future, require some assumptions that can only be estimates. Moreover, in present practice, budget projections for more than a year or two ahead regularly assume conditions that are considered to be desirable and hoped to be achievable.

No future path of the economy can be probable if it is not consistent with the goals of the Federal Reserve. Or to put it another way, the most probable path of the economy is the path the Federal Reserve is seeking to achieve. Of course, there will be deviations, even substantial ones, from the Federal Reserve's target path, but that target is the most probable future path. The budget plan should thus be consistent with the Federal Reserve's objectives. A budget plan that aims to achieve a surplus of a specified size if the economy moves on a path that the Federal Reserve does not intend to finance is unrealistic. This fact is recognized to a small degree in present procedures. When the Federal Reserve makes its reports to Congress (as required by the Humphrey-Hawkins Act), it is required to indicate how its forecast conforms with the assumptions the administration uses for its budget. The Federal Reserve treats this requirement very cautiously. It never extends its forecast more than one year into the future. It never acknowledges that its forecast is a target of monetary policy, although that is certainly implied. That is, if the forecast path of the economy was not what the Federal Reserve considered desirable, it would presumably have chosen a different monetary policy. Moreover, since the forecast is confined to the short-term future, the range of eligible forecasts is usually not very great, so it always turns out that the administration's assumptions lie within the range of the Federal Reserve's forecasts.

The Federal Reserve should be required to state an economic target for the four years of the budget planning period contemplated in the reform proposal made here. The administration and the Congress should base their budget plans on economic assumptions that are consistent with the Federal Reserve's target.

The Federal Reserve should set forth a medium-term—say four-year—target for a nominal variable. This could be either a measure of the price level or a measure of nominal income, such as GNP in current dollars. The economic assumptions underlying the four-year budget framework should be consistent with the Federal Reserve's target. Of course, this single variable, whether a price-level variable or a nominal-income variable, is not a sufficient specification of economic assumptions from which to estimate budget outcomes. There will have to be calculations of a number of other variables—real output, employment and unemployment, interest rates, and some aspects of the distribution of income. However, the Federal Reserve's target will serve to constrain the estimates of the other variables. It will be a constraint established by a fairly objective body and so will reduce the possibility of manipulating the economic assumptions to serve the convenience of the administration or the Congress, and reduce the controversy about the assumptions.

The Federal Reserve will, of course, resist this proposal. It will not like the implication of responsibility and accountability that goes with it. But a clear statement of Federal Reserve targets is important for reasons other than its contribution to budget planning. Private decisionmakers base their actions on expectations about what the Federal Reserve will do. These decisions will be most likely to stabilize the economy around the path the Federal Reserve desires if the Federal Reserve has made its intentions clear. Moreover, having a publicly known medium-term goal will increase the Federal Reserve's flexibility to deal with short-term situations. When its medium-term intentions are unclear, any short-term adaptation can be misinterpreted by markets as a sign of what the longer-term goals are. One example of this appeared after the stock market crash of October 1987. Many people were concerned that an injection of liquidity to stabilize the situation would be taken to mean that the Federal Reserve had embarked upon a more inflationary course for the longer-term future. Having a well-known medium-term goal will help to make the Federal Reserve's own actions as well as the behavior of private parties more stabilizing. The point is that the Federal Reserve should announce some target or targets and that the budget estimates should be consistent with that target.

The idea that the administration and the Congress should be bound by the targets of this quasi-independent agency may seem odd. But the present situation is even odder. When the Office of Management and Budget or the Congressional Budget Office undertakes to produce the economic assumptions underlying the budget, it knows that to a large degree it is implicitly forecasting what the Federal Reserve is going to do. In the proposal made here the budget-makers would explicitly ask the Federal Reserve what its intentions are and accept the achievement of those intentions as the most probable outcome. If that is too much authority to give a quasi-independent agency, it raises a question about whether the agency should be as independent as it is. Certainly it is making many other decisions that are just as critical for the economy.

The proposal, then, visualizes the president submitting a four-year budget framework using economic assumptions consistent with the Federal Reserve's target. The path of the deficit or surplus in this framework should meet two conditions. First, the aggregate surplus or deficit for the period should be consistent with the president's objective for the share of the national output to be devoted to saving and investment. Second, its size should be a constant as the economy moves along the assumed economic path or, if that is not possible, should change gradually and steadily from year to year. Congress would act upon the four-year budget subject to the same conditions.

This proposal is a long way from the simplicity of the postwar rule that the budget should be balanced at high employment. But that simplicity was an illusion. It did not consider that the actual size of the deficit or surplus realized over a period of years would be a matter of importance. It did not consider that the desired size of the surplus or deficit was not a constant but might change as the weight given to savings and investment changed. It did not consider the problem of making a transition to the desired size of surplus or deficit if the economy were off the desired path.

The problem with the postwar rule was that it was too simple for the real world yet too complicated to have general appeal. This means economists can either go to a simpler and possibly more intuitively appealing rule—like "balancing the budget"—which is even less realistic than the postwar rule, or to a rule that is more difficult to describe, enforce, and explain but will yield better results if followed. The proposal here is for the latter.

In fact, some of the qualifications to the postwar rule that are incorporated in this proposal were allowed for in the CED statement of 1947. Notably, that statement said there should be a small surplus in the budget at high employment, which should be constant unless "there is a major change in the condition of national life." This qualification was the contribution of Beardsley Ruml, a very wise man. The qualification he had in mind was that a surplus might turn out to be inconsistent with the achievement of high employment, for essentially "stagnationist" reasons. But it does leave room for the point made here, that from the standpoint of economic growth, the desirable size of surplus or deficit changes from time to time. Similarly, the CED left room for departing from the target high-employment surplus in extraordinary conditions, but it did not deal with the problem of getting back to the target surplus after the departure. So what may seem to be an abandonment of the postwar rule could be interpreted as only spelling out its implications.

The strategy recommended here implies that fluctuations in the size of the deficit or surplus, associated with fluctuations in the economy, will be accepted—that no attempt will be made to offset them—but that neither will there (ordinarily) be any move to vary the budget position beyond this automatic response in an effort to counter actual or forecast economic fluctuations. Some analysts fear that because of the size of recent and present deficits, any increase connected with another recession could not be tolerated, or if tolerated would have a destabilizing effect. There is a kernel of validity in this. If a substantial increase in the deficit in a recession were taken as a sign that future debt levels would be much higher than previously expected, there might be an immediate interest-rate-raising effect that would impede recovery. This possibility does not make it desirable, or even feasible, to avoid an increase of the deficit in a recession. It does emphasize the importance of having and carrying out a policy that reduces deficits in recoveries and gives reasonable assurance that the long-run path of the debt will not be greatly disturbed by short-run fluctuations of the economy.

Notes

Chapter 2

1. Arthur Smithies, *The Budgetary Process in the United States* (New York: McGraw-Hill, 1955), p. 117.

2. Reprinted in Arthur Smithies and Gerard R. Butters, eds., *Readings in Fiscal Policy* (Homewood, Ill.: Richard D. Irwin, 1955), p. 365. This statement was drafted by me, a point worth mentioning, since the present analysis and recommendations may suggest ignorance of the argument made in 1947.

3. Smithies, *Budgetary Process*, pp. 83-84.

4. The commission report and the Denison-Stein paper can be found in *Goals for Americans* (Englewood Cliffs, N.J.: Prentice-Hall, 1960).

5. In his 1963 Ely Lecture of the American Economic Association, Professor Tobin further developed the idea that the size of the surplus should be regarded as a policy instrument for affecting total saving and investment.

I was a discussant of that lecture and dissented on the grounds that the rate of total saving and investment was none of the government's business. I have modified that position since, as is clear in this book. Tobin's original article was "Growth Through Taxation," *New Republic*, July 25, 1960. The Ely Lecture is in the *American Economic Review* 54, no. 3 (1963).

6. See, for example, remarks of Congressman Trent Lott in *Crisis in the Budget Process* (Washington, D.C.: American Enterprise Institute for Public Policy Research, 1985).

7. See, for example, Allen Schick in *Crisis in the Budget Process*, ibid.

Chapter 3
1. Robert Barro, "Are Government Bonds Net Wealth?" *Journal of Political Economy* 82, no. 6 (1974), pp. 1095–1117.

Chapter 5
1. "Discriminate Deterrence" (Report of the Commission on Integrated Long-Term Strategy, Washington, D.C., January 1988), p. 59. The commission was chaired by Fred C. Ikle and Albert Wohlstetter. Since the commission consisted of experts on strategy, not on the growth rate of the economy, I consider their recommendation to be for a 3 percent annual increase of real defense expenditures, not for devoting a constant share of GNP to defense, which is a slightly different thing.

2. Professor Martin Feldstein has recently presented estimates that substantial reduction of the budget deficit would substantially reduce interest *rates* and so contribute to solving the budget problem (*Wall Street Journal*, May 15, 1988). I cannot check on the validity of his estimates, and I have not included that in my calculations. The reduction of budget costs that would result from a decline of interest rates is sometimes regarded as a windfall that relieves the budget and hurts no one. That is a mistake: all recipients of interest on the federal debt would bear the cost of this relief to the budget.

Chapter 6
1. See U.S. Congress, Joint Committee on the Economic Report, Subcommittee on Monetary, Credit, and Fiscal Policies (Douglas Subcommittee), *Report*, 81st Cong., 2d sess., 1950; The President's Cabinet Committee on Price Stability for Economic Growth, *Managing Our Money, Our Budget, and Our Debt*, October 25, 1959; and Milton Friedman, "A Monetary and Fiscal Framework for Economic Stability," *American Economic Review*, 1948.

2. Paul A. Samuelson, "Principles and Rules in Modern Fiscal Policy: A Neo-Classical Reformulation," in *Money, Trade and Economic Growth: Essays in Honor of John Henry Williams* (New York: Macmillan Co., 1951), pp. 173-74.

Index